"WAzzup?"
Rich Wasmer
06/2015

WHENEVER ROTARY SCOUTS FALL IN LINE

"As I begin my Scouting career"…
Midland Park, New Jersey 1950

RICH WASMER

ISBN: 978-1-4834-2979-3 (sc)
ISBN: 978-1-4834-2978-6 (e)

Lulu Publishing Services rev. date: 6/11/2015

Preface

"Whenever Rotary scouts fall in line, we're going to have a ripping roaring time," are the beginning of the lyrics to a camp song that many of us have been accustomed to singing for decades as we lined up for meal times at the Dining Hall. Singing that song is one of the fine memories of a camp that all of us have shared. This book, more than four years in the preparation, is a long overdue publication. I believe the only other book on Camp Rotary was published in 1967 which dealt with its history. This book is so much more. Not only does it bring us up to date on the by-gone days of a great scout camp, and our O.A. Lodges, It also includes some of my classic campfire stories, plus the most terrifying tale ever told around a Camp Rotary camp fire, the John, the Hannibal, Potter saga; a story of two legends, Marv and Justine Valentine and me, in an era when many Camp Rotary traditions began, and a chapter on a neighboring rival scout camp, Lost Lake Scout Reservation, with an incredible history of its properties. Since August of 1925, when Camp Rotary first opened its gates to scout camping, thousands upon thousands of scouts have been falling in line to experience an adventure second to none at one of the most highly regarded scout camps in the Nation. Its' 1100 plus acres hold a special place in our hearts. To those of us who have experienced the sights and sounds of this dynamic, and awesome outdoor facility, we have come to realize that there is no other scout camp quite like Camp Rotary. Many of us have wonderful memories that never can be erased, and I have been privileged to have spent more than forty summers, either as a scout leader or staff member, telling campfire tales at the camp's eleven different camp sites to troops throughout Michigan, the United States and Canada. It has been those troops and their members, the scouts and adult leaders who have battery charged me, and kept me going for so long for which I am forever grateful. And they have urged me on to write this book. I do hope "Whenever Rotary Scouts Fall in Line" meets or exceeds your expectations.

Rich Wasmer

"WAZZZZUUUP?"

Acknowledgements

Erv Hutter (Eagle Scout) for relating his knowledge of Camp Rotary's and the Order of the Arrow's history along with his camp experiences. This former staffer and I go back to the time when he was OA Tobico Chapter Chief and I his Chapter Advisor. We also took our OA Vigil together at Camp Rotary.

Camp Rotary Camp Director, (Eagle Scout) Andrew Wright, for relating his experiences and contributions. When I served on Rotary Staff back in 2003, Andrew was a young, energetic C.I.T. Andrew originated the cover to this book.

Retired Public Safety Officer and former staffer (Eagle Scout) Gary Valentine, Son of Camp Rotary legends, Marv and Justine Valentine, for his personal reflections.

Former Camp Rotary Camp Director, (Eagle Scout) Brad Murray, for his outstanding council and camping leadership and unending support. His hard work and dedication kept Rotary going in the right direction.

Except where credited, the contents of this book and its views, opinions, impressions, storylines and photographs are those of the authors or contributors and should not infringe upon the rights of any author, photographer, composer or publisher.

DEDICATED TO
SUZANNE M. WASMER
1971 – 2008
"Her passion was catching the
"big-ones" in Beebe Lake."

AND ALL
CAMP ROTARY STAFF AND VOLUNTEERS
PAST – PRESENT – FUTURE

"Let us be diligent in safe-guarding the values and ideals of the Boy Scouts of America and not be led in directions that would deviate us from the Scout Oath and Scout Law."

.......The Author

The Bay City Times, "People's Forum," December 14, 1993.

"I would like to respond to "God and Boy Scout's Honor," by Marianne Means, New York Times News Service. (Opinions, Dec. 9). She says it's legally correct but morally indefensible with the recent Supreme Court's decision on allowing Boy Scouts of America to ban boys who refuse to take an oath to God. Ms. Means states it is entirely possible to be a "decent person of honorable character who knows the difference between right and wrong, and still have doubts about the concept of God."

This might be entirely possible in Ms. Means' view, but not mine. The chances of a young person not being of honorable character are greater if he/she has doubts about the reality of God. What's to stop the growing number of our young people turning to a life of crime? Society? Certainly not in a Godless environment. God fearing youngsters not only are more apt to be decent citizens of honorable character, knowing the difference between right and wrong, they will also practice right over wrong.

The Supreme Court decision was a correct and moral one. The Cub Scout Promise and the Boy Scout Oath to God must remain intact. Otherwise there would be no foundation to any of Scouting's values".

Rich Wasmer, SM, Troop 103, Bay City, MI.

Contents

How Our Camp Rotary Campsites Were Named

By Erv Hutter

CURTIS – In honor of Albert Frederick Curtis, the first Council Executive with the Saginaw Council, 1918.

JAMES WEST – In honor of James Ellis West, the first Chief Scout Executive of The Boy Scouts of America from 1911 – 1943.

SCHUCK – In honor of Arthur Aloys Schuck, Third Chief Scout Executive of the Boy Scouts of America, 1948 – 1960.

BRADEN – In honor of Frank Walter Braden, Director of Region 7, 1948 – 1968 and friend of Camp Rotary.

BURROWS – Named for George Lord Burrows III, Saginaw, MI., dedicated community volunteer and Rotary Club Trustee. A member of the "Committee of 300" that founded Delta College in 1961.

UNCLE OTTO – Named for Otto Caspar Hornung, Detroit, MI. Formed the first Boy Scout troop in North America (Troop 1, Auburn, N.Y.) Internationally known as a showman of various feats of Scout Craft skills.

BADEN-POWELL – Robert Stephenson Smyth Baden-Powell, first Baron Baden-Powell; B-P or Lord Baden-Powell. A lieutenant-General in the British Army, Writer and Founder of the Scout movement.

RANGER – This is the only camp site not named for a person. Dedicated to the memory of all our year-round Rangers who have maintained Rotary for so many years. Ranger Whitey Wilcox, Ranger Marv Valentine, and Ranger Art (Bear) Beck are just three of them.

FRETWELL – For Elbert Kirtley Fretwell, second Chief Scout Executive of the Boy Scouts of America, 1943 – 1948

DAN BOONE – Daniel Boone, an American Pioneer, Explorer and Frontiersman whose frontier exploits made him one of the first heroes of the United States.

FORT SCOTT – Named for W. Emerson Scott who was a dedicated scouter and Explorer from Caro, MI. An Adventurer best known for his canoe trip from Ojibwa Island in Saginaw, MI. to the Arctic Circle.

Camp Directors of Camp Rotary

Compiled by Erv Hutter

1925 –	O. L. Duggan
1926 – 1927 –	Guy Goddard
1928 – 1929 –	William Morgan
1930 – 1931 –	Evan Price
1932 –	Glenn Uggen
1933 –	Harry Nagel
1934 – 1939 –	J Hebert Saum
1940 –	Ralph Van Volkinburg
1941 – 1942 –	Max Clark
1943 –	E. B. Clark
1944 –	Emil Pfister
1945 – 1947 –	Clifford Klapp
1948 –	Lester Eyre
1949 – 1950 –	Harold Oatley
1951 – 1953 –	Ken Poulson
1954 – 1955 –	William Doser
1956 –	Bernard Toland
1957 –	Everett Vincent
1958 –	Edward Goetz
1959 –	Jack Scheall
1960 – 1961 –	Max Grove
1962 – 1963 –	Allen Fennell
1964 – 1965 –	Robert Koenemann

1966 – 1967 –	Dorm Gothup
1968 –	Ronald Artecki
1969 -	Robert Koenemann
1970 –	Jim MacTavish
1971 –	Ron White
1972 –	Larry Smith
1973 – 1999 –	Marv Valentine
2000 – 2007 –	Ed Houlehan
2008 – 2014 -	Brad Murray
2015 –	Andrew Wright

CHAPTER 1

THE ON-GOING HISTORY OF CAMP ROTARY

By Erv Hutter

For more than 40 years I've had the privilege of tramping the trails Camp Rotary. I've had the pleasure to experience a whole lot of adventure around the banks of Lake Beebe, but I've also met many guys who were there long before me, and I've listened to their tales as well. Most of this stuff has been gathering dust in my old head for too many years. I first drove into the gates of camp in August 1972 as a Webelos Scout attending family Camp. My first summer as a camper was 1974. I started serving on camp staffs in 1976 as a C.I.T., and 1978 as a regular staff member. At that time there were still old-timers around who had been on staff in the 30's and 40's. I was always interested in camp history and got lots of information from them, and through other sources through the years. Now I guess I'm the old timer. So it is time to pass on some of what I know to y'all. Remember, these are my impressions, so others may be different.

The Rotary Hilton and Old Dining Hall

I thought I'd start with a building that is near and dear to my heart. I lived in this cabin called the "Rotary Hilton" for two years, year round. Even during the snows of winter. The paper thin walls did little to keep out the cold, but I survived, along with all my little rodent friends that shared the cabin with me, trying to stay warm.

The "Hilton" was built in 1925 and thus was one of the original structures on the property. It was built to house the kitchen staff. I'm told from staff members from the 1930's that it held six staff members, with two three-tiered bunk beds. The kitchen staff needed to report by 5 A.M. so they needed to be close to the kitchen. It was also close enough to go nod off for a nap in the mid afternoon. The old dining hall (now the trading post and pavilion) was right next door with the camp office and quartermaster shack right across the street. The main camp area was centered on this part of camp. The boat house was just down the hill (now the platform for the campfire bowl) but there was no path down past the Hilton, access was from the lakeshore trail. Also right there was the central latrine and ice-house. The latrine part of the building was torn down in 1982, but hadn't been used as such for about four years before that. The ice house still exists, but was taken to a neighboring property in 2008. The Hilton was demolished in early 2008 to make way for the new campfire amphitheater tail. –RIP-

The Saginaw Boy Scout Council with the assistance of key members of the Saginaw Rotary Club searched for a permanent summer camp property for Saginaw area Scouts in 1923 and 1924. In early 1924, a location on Beebe Lake in Hatton Township, Clare County was found. The Rotary Club put an option on the land in early fall of 1924 and the land was officially purchased in 1925.

The old dining hall was also built in 1925 in preparation for Camp Kepayshowink's official move from Arnold Lake to Beebe Lake. Before Camp Rotary, scouts attended scout camp at "Camp Kepayshowink" on Arnold Lake six miles north of Harrison, MI. In 1925, the last Boy Scout encampment at Arnold Lake consisted of four weeks. The first three weeks were camped at Arnold Lake and the last one at Camp Rotary. The scout paid $8.00 per week to camp. Rotary's first full summer camping season was in 1926. Old pictures of the dining hall show a classic Boy Scout camp dining hall. An Indian War Canoe hung from the rafters and Troop, Patrol and Jamboree flags hung all around the place. It was a seasonal building with screen windows and propped-up wooden shutters. The fireplace never worked too well, the draft wasn't built right and so smoke would come back into the building. A pathway led directly up to the main doors from the parade field (now the back doors of the trading post). Pine trees were planted on the hillside in the early 1950's to reduce the erosion caused by hundreds of scouts going up and down the hill. The dining hall became too small for the growing camp and was torn down in 1971 when the new facility, the Central Dining Hall, was built on the opposite side of the parade field. With the old dining hall, only the foundation remained until 1979 when the "Roy Chase Memorial Building" was built. This honored the former Lodge Advisor of Kepayshowink and Mischigonong Lodge 89. The building was designed for a camp trading post with storage room and the OA Room, a room for the OA ceremonial team to keep their gear in, year-round storage of OA gear and material, as well as a changing area in preparation for the Calling-Out Ceremony on Friday evenings. Camp OA election records were also kept here by the Camp OA Chief. The money to build this building as well as the pavilion roof over the rest of the old dining hall foundation was raised by the OA Lodge as a memorial to their late advisor. Very quickly however the original purpose of the building and especially the OA Room became lost. By 1980 this had become the Ski Room in the off season and by the mid 1980's the OA did not have access to this room. It was for a while turned into an extension of the trading post where slushies' and candy were sold and then into the handicraft room. The dedication plaque to Roy Chase was never placed on the building. A new roof was placed on the building and pavilion in 2007 and the top of the fireplace stack was removed.

Scout Craft Skill Center

The area today called the Scout Craft Area, started out as the camp parking lot. My good old friend, Mike Murphy, who was on staff from 1970-76 and 1979 told me that until around 1970 the Scout Craft Area was kind of spread out on the flat area north of Carney Health Lodge. By my first summer as a Scout in 1974, it was pretty well established and was called the Scout Craft Skill Center or SCSC for short. Kevin Henika and Mike Murphy changed the name of the Scout Craft Area to the Scout Craft Skill Center or SCSC in 1974. Murphy chain sawed a chunk of log with the initials.

This was always my favorite area of camp. It was hands on. We got to build really big projects with logs and rope. Some of my favorites included the Monkey Bridge and Signal Tower. The Monkey Bridge was 110 foot long and 15 feet in the air. It started in SCSC with an "A" frame and proceeded across the obstacle course Dust Valley over to a tree with a "Y" in it. We had a safety line above it and ran open times for Scouts to cross it. It really brought the Scouts into our area.

The Signal Tower was 35 foot tall at its top platform. I wanted to build something permanent, so we selectively cut some oak trees from the oak forest north and east of the gravel pit in North Camp. It was a monster to build and took most of the staff to lift it after we built it on its side during staff week 1980. I bought a cowbell and put it on a 10-foot pole above the top platform. Of course scouts always wanted to climb it, so we started the policy that a scout could climb it and ring the bell for each merit badge they completed in camp. "Just bring your signed blue-card and you can "TIME THE CLOWER AND BING THE RELL!" Both the Tower and the Monkey Bridge were up year-round for about 8 years when the BSA changed the rules and took some of the adventure out of scouting by saying that monkey bridges couldn't be more than 3-foot off the ground unless you had a certified COPE Director running it.

In 75' and 76' Murphy had a program called the Skill Wagon. It was a small Conestoga-type wagon that was taken from campsite to campsite on a schedule and a staff member or C.I.T. from SCSC would teach basic skills right in the campsite. "Totin' Chip," fire building and the likes were taught. I revived the program in 1980 through 1982.

One of the best area promotions that ever happened again, happened in 1980. That year Marv Valentine, Camp Director, bought a number of different colored Camp Rotary hats that were available in the Trading Post. So, Tim "Hubba Bubba" Schreiner, the Waterback Director, and I came up with a plan that each program area would sport a different colored hat.

Waterback had red, SCSC blue and white, Nature green, Field Sports blue and gold, etc. We made quite a production out of it. Bubba had some kind of a beachfront ceremony for all those scouts who bought red hats. I would let the blue and white hats "Time the Clower and bing the rell" and so on. The result was that the scouts really got into it. Each hat was only $5. Marv had to reorder hats several times during the summer. Red ones went the best, even though I'd never admit it at the time. For several years after that I'd see those hats everywhere. In 1984 when I was a student at MSU, I even saw several on campus.

One of the things that SCSC was famous for was all of the tents and dining-flies. There was no pavilion there until 1985 so we had to set things up ourselves. I personally liked it better that way. Each year we could make changes. Each merit badge area had its own dining fly. We built what some people called the pregnant watermelon. It was supposed to be a Woodland Indian styled wigwam. We built it according to directions in the Ben Hunt Indian Craft Book, and placed it just across the road (on the Deer Lodge side of the road), and made an Indian Village. And it looked great, accept when it came to covering it, we used old red-tag-tents; wall tents that were ripped or dry rot. So it was green! It was very useful. We set up a small tipi there and a big tipi on Indian Point in the middle grounds of Lake Beebe. Indian Lore Merit Badge became very popular and during Cub Day Camp it was a great program feature.

Cooking Merit Badge was always something of a challenge at Rotary. Marv was pretty tight with the program budget. So in the early years Scouts really didn't learn to cook that much. In fact one of the meals I remember that was served was baloney sandwiches! We changed that in the 80's by doing real menu planning and working with the business Manager and Dining Hall Steward to have well balanced menus that actually had to be cooked. Cooking Merit Badge had been assigned to a C.I.T. or one of the first year Camp Staff, but when I was SCSC Director, I took it myself. It was really fun and I learned a lot about outdoor cooking and hopefully the Scouts did too.

Overnight camping was always a great part of the SCSC program. There was the Indian Lore overnight that was on Indian point. Some years it was just the scouts and a staff member, and usually a C.I.T. going over and camping under the stars, but other years we set up a large tipi and built another wigwam on Indian Point. One year, I believe in 1990, Austen Brauker who is an Odawa, built a sweat lodge on the point. It was great. We'd put large rocks in the campfire and then brought them into the sweat lodge and pour water on them, then afterwards go jump in the lake.

1976 was the first year Wilderness Survival was offered at camp because it was a new merit badge that year. In those first years the requirements stated that all you could take with you on the overnight were a jackknife and a survival kit that would fit in a film cylinder. Everything we ate for dinner, we found in nature. We'd fish by the dam. The pan fish were so plentiful that we'd drop a bare hook on a stick and line into the water and caught enough for supper. We ate edible wild plants. It was fun and we learned a lot. It was also through this overnight that I got recommended to be a C.I.T. in 1976.

The Shoults Pavilion was built in SCSC in 1986 as a memorial to Jeff "Bings" Shoults, the SCSC Director in 1983 and was scheduled to be the director again in 1984, but he died from cancer just before the season started. His home Troop 387 from Saginaw raised the funds and built the pavilion in his memory. "Bings" was a good kid, and a dependable staff leader, he is still missed today. While I personally really don't care for the pavilion, every time I see it I think of "Bings." During the winter we would flood the area under the pavilion for an ice skating rink. With the lights, scouts could skate into the night.

One great program in the 1970s and 1980s that centered in SCSC was the Pioneer Camp Program. Older Scouts would sign up for this from Monday through Thursday. They would go out to North Camp just past where the football field is now, to the old hand pump site. There they would work on building a log cabin. They worked on other merit badges like Pioneering, Cooking and Orienteering as well. The cabin was worked on over four summers but never got a roof on it. It was built out of poplar and just rotted out after a few years. You can't even see the remnants today.

For me the Scout Craft Area offered the adventure we advertise in scouting. There are tons of short cuts that can be taken in presenting the program as we've seen through the years, but it can also be adventurous. One can do back-country survival camping in a summer camp context. One can learn the ways, and traditions of the Native Americans, knots and lashings and pioneering projects can be bigger than life, and fun and exciting. Orienteering and hiking can take in the whole 1180 acres of camp property.

ORDER OF THE ARROW

Most of you guys are arrow-men and know at least a bit about the Order of the Arrow, how it was started at the Philadelphia Council Camp called Treasure Island in 1915 by its Camp Director Urner Goodman, and Assistant Camp Director Carroll Edson. I had the opportunity to go to Treasure Island in 1980 for the 65th Anniversary of the founding. Goodman had just died the previous year and Edson was so old that they just pushed him around in a wheelchair. He died a few years later in 1986. I'm told that this was his last appearance at an OA event. Anyway, as usual, I digress. In 1948 the OA became an official part of the Boy Scout program, although there were other camp honor organizations that were also in existence like the Fire Crafters, the tribe of Gimogash, Mic-O-Say and literally a dozen others.

The tribe of Gimogash was introduced into the old Saginaw Council in the spring of 1920. Scout Executive A.F. Curtis took one adult and 6 Scouts to Toledo for the original induction. Exactly how many years it stayed in Saginaw, no one now knows, but it was around for a least several years. Wayne Dancer, an early Kepayshowink camp staffer was a member and is thought to have helped start a chapter in the Bay City Council (later Summer Trails Council). The Summer Trails Tribe later became the Gimogash Lodge of the Order of the Arrow. Their lodge emblem is now the most collectible scouting patch ever. With only a handful of known patches they have gone for as high as $24,000 on eBay.

In 1936 Camp Director Herb Saum did begin using the Order of the Arrow program at Camp Kepayshowink. In fact the lodge was called Kepayshowink Lodge number 89. Through most of its history the Order of the Arrow was a camp-based organization. In the early days, camp sessions were for two-weeks rather than one week and the Ordeal was actually done right in camp during the session. The OA was an integral part of the camp. They built much of the infrastructure of the place. They laid water lines, built latrines, built the dam, built the waterfront retaining wall, etc.

One of the major projects they engaged in, in the later 1940-50's was the planting of literally thousands of pine trees. If you've ever noticed when you come into camp all the trees that seem to be in straight rows, that's because they are. They were planted. Much of the main camp area was open when the camp was purchased from the Pinehurst Orchard Resort Association in 1924. The area had been logged very heavily, in fact there is only a couple known virgin white pine trees remaining on the 1180 acres of camp property. So the camp had to be reforested.

Another area of reforestation was the area on the east side of the parade field going up the hill to the old mess hall, now the trading post. The Order did most of this planting.

Herb Saum started the Kepayshowink Lodge in 1936, but when he left Valley Trails Council in 1939, the lodge did as well. During the World War II years it was difficult to get older staff members and the OA was just dormant. In either 1942 or 1943 a volunteer named Harold Oatley, who was Dean of Boys in the Cass City School District, was instrumental in resurrecting Kepayshowink Lodge. Within a few years it was again a vibrant program at Camp Rotary.

The old Kepayshowink ceremony bowl was on the south side of the lake. It still exists in the woods, but you have to know what you're looking for to find it. During the time I was Lodge Chief in 1979-80, we had so many new ordeal candidates that it required two separate ceremony locations. We rebuilt and re-used the old ceremony bowl as well as the new one on Indian Point that was built in the mid 1960's.

As Scout Councils split and merged in the 1950's through the 1970's so did the OA lodges. Kepayshowink lodge 89 existed from 1936-1971 (with the exception of 1939-42). Gimogash Lodge 273 of the Summer Trails Council existed from 1942-1961 when it merged into Kepayshowink as Summer Trails merged with Valley Trails Council to become Saginaw Bay Area Council. Gimogash had split in 1951 when the Paul Bunyan Council split off of Summer Trails and Tittabawasink Lodge was formed. It existed from 1951-71 when Paul Bunyan merged with Saginaw Bay Area to form Lake Huron Area Council and Mischigonong Lodge.

While Kepayshowink was operating in Camp Rotary and Bear Lake during the 1960's, when Mischigonong formed in 1971, it operated in three summer camps, with the addition of Paul Bunyan Scout Reservation.

The Kepayshowink Lodge calling out ceremony was one of the best I've seen in the country. It was the public persona of the Order of the Arrow. Each Friday night, the arrow-men would call out new members at the campfire bowl. In the early days, candidates would be stripped to their waist as they approached Allowat Sakima for tapping out. While this was modified in later years, the tap-out was a very impressive ceremony. In the mid 1980's when women officially became members of the OA, the tap-out portion of the ceremony was banished.

From the early 1950's through the mid 1980's the ceremonial team wore Plains Indian garb. Allowat Sakima wore a long trailered bonnet with green and white feathers. Meteu, the medicine man, wore a horned bonnet with a trailer. Nutiket and Kitchkinet also wore full bonnets, but without trailers. The principals wore grease paint to help hide their true identities. Allowat had a yellow lightning bolt across his face with black and white face paint covering the rest. Meteu quartered his face with black and white paint. Nutiket and Kitchkinet halved their faces with red and white and blue and white paint. The Drummer, canoeing jives and land jives usually wore only breechcloth and face paint.

In the 1980's there was a new sensitivity to Native American cultures and face paint became *verboten*. Woodland styles of dress were adopted, which were closer to the garb that would have been worn by Natives who camped at Camp Rotary prior to European intervention.

Over the years the Order of the Arrow has become less and less of a camp-based program. While the Order still does service projects at camp, they are no longer an integral part of the program. Each summer there is a Camp Chief that coordinates unit elections and calling out ceremonies. I served in that capacity from 1978-82 (and at Bear Lake in 1983). The Camp Director doesn't have a say about who the Camp Chief is. And while Marv Valentine certainly made his ideas clear as to how the ceremony should go during his tenure, the OA, in my opinion, is more of a foreign organization than it was originally designed to be. This is not a Lake Huron Area Council thing, but is kind of the nature of the beast becoming more of a senior scout program than an honor camper society. However, it has been and continues to be a dynamic program within the Boy Scouts of America.

NATURE AREA

The area of camp that is now the Nature area used to be a campsite pre 1965-ish. It was one of the original troop sites as best I can tell. Up until the late 1940's most scouts came to camp individually, what we today call provisional camping. The camp provided all the camp leadership. There was Boone and Roosevelt, Forrester and Seton. Each Camp Site had its own identifying color of neckerchief. Scouts usually came up for two-week periods. They'd take the train from Saginaw to Clare, and then hike from the Clare depot the 7 miles up to camp.

The current Nature area was originally Boone Campsite. Later the name was changed to Uncle Otto, named after the famed Detroit area Scouter—Otto Hornung. Hornung was nationally famous for his trick campfire lighting among many other things. He would build a fire lay, and then using flint, and steel start the fire from yards away just by target shooting the spark into the right place. My old Scoutmaster told me that at the 1960 National Scout Jamboree, President Eisenhower took time to watch this amazing feat. Waz' remembers meeting Uncle Otto at a Council Camporee in the Midland County Fairgrounds in the mid 1960's. Uncle Otto had many Scouting artifacts on displayed in the old church building on the grounds. Among his artifacts were his fantastic collection of knives and to prove how sharp he kept them, he gave Waz' an extremely cleaned dry shave that he's never forgotten.

Anyway in 1964-65 the campsite places were changed to their current configuration and Boone and Uncle Otto were names given to other sites. (The Scout Craft Skill Center sign was routed into the backside of the old Forrester campsite sign). This left the area open for other uses. I'm not sure which year this area was officially first used as the nature area, but by the time I got to camp in 1974 it was well established.

In the 1970's the name of the area was changed from Nature-Ecology to Eco-Trip. The name lasted only a few years but was part of the distinctive area names that came out of the 1970's including SCSC and Waterback.

One summer (1975) there was a totally blind man that was on staff who led the blind nature hikes and set up the first "spider web" to develop seminary perception. His name was Russ Zimmermann, and years later I ran into him again. When he was at camp he had just graduated from seminary. He was an ordained Lutheran Minister. He's now retired but when he retired I was at seminary, and I bought many of his books.

In 1976 two Scouts from Troop 313 in Saginaw did their Eagle project in camp establishing a nature trail with stations marking the different types of flora, and eco-systems. I wish I remembered what their names were, there used to be a plaque at the beginning of the trail, but that is now long gone. I remember their Scoutmaster, Harold Schmidt, and a great Scouter who contributed much time to camp. The nature trail is still there, but has of course changed over the years.

One of the features I remember best was the "Hotel." It was a multi-room HUMONGOUS tent that was used as the Nature HQ. The Nature Director in 1974 was Jack Morse, a professor from Mid-Michigan Community College. He was my first merit badge counselor-Astronomy MB. I remember the week that I took it, I was the only Scout in the class. Gabriel Kunje, the International Scout from Guyana assisted Jack for the night time star observations. They set up a telescope in the Waterback tower and we identified planets and constellations, and even satellites going by. It is still one of the best places I know of for star study. Then I had to walk back to Boone Campsite by myself. I was 11 and really scared. When I got just past the old water tower there was a tree that was in the middle of the road almost to Fretwell Campsite, well, of course, I smacked right into the tree, and broke my glasses. I've smacked into more than one tree over the years, but now can still walk almost anywhere in camp without a flashlight. One summer I took my son and two others on a hike around the lake without a flashlight, and still could do it with no problems.

As usual I digress. In the summer of 1980, the current Nature Center was built, a gift from Downtown Saginaw Rotary Club. The dedication for the building was on my 18th birthday-October 14, 1980. Marv asked me to cut the rope (instead of a ribbon) for the event. The thing I remember the most is that we had a huge early snow storm that year on that date. Here were all these suits from Saginaw in their patent leather shoes trudging through 2 foot of snow for the ceremony. I went to cut the rope with an ax from the QM, but unfortunately Art "Bear" Beck brought the dullest ax in camp and it took about 10 chops to finally break through the rope. The Nature Center was rededicated to the memory of one of those "suits" - Max

Heavenrich, a dedicated Rotarian and supporter of Camp Rotary for many years.

There are so many great staffers I remember from the Nature area: Denny Tompkins, Jim "Froggenheimer" Brauker, the Faller Twins, Stew "Grizzly" Beach, Wally Ewing, Eric Tanner, Ron "Aunt Jemima" Smith, Phyliss "Mother Nature" Vaughn," "Jukebox George" Hutter, Mike "Bike" Falardeau, Marc Hendricks, Joe Lapard, and Marc Beaudin to name just a few.

There was actually a whole day that I was acting nature director. In the summer of 1981 during our smallest week of camp that year, a flu epidemic broke out. Nearly everyone in camp including staff and Scouts got it. There was puke everywhere. The only people on senior staff that didn't get it were Marv, Tom Oleniacz and I. So for a whole day, Marv ran Waterback, Tom SCSC and I ran Nature. The ranges were closed, as were the Trading Post and QM. Luckily by the end of the week everyone had recovered. We were never sure if it was actually the flu or food poisoning, but it was probably the flu, because we didn't all get it at the same time.

I remember Denny Tompkins telling me when I took Environmental Science that the whole camp was the Nature area, that the Eco-Trip was just the interpretation area. I remember all those weekly Critter Crawls. The big snapping turtle with the missing right front leg; he got himself caught just about every week for at least 10 summers in a row. And I remember Stew and Stub Patterson bringing up all those geese in the pen.

SCOUT P.A.T.H.

Many of the old-timers won't know of this area of camp. It was brand new in 1990. I developed this program after nearly 15 years of camp experience. I saw the need to have a First Year program and had seen a number of different programs at scout camps around the Mid-West. But this program I developed was unique to Camp Rotary.

The basic premise behind the program was to teach first year campers all of the skills required to earn their First-Class, as well as to get them acclimated to camp. Attrition rates in scouting during the 1980's were getting really bad. We already knew that if a Scout didn't go the summer camp his first year, after crossing into the troop, that nearly 80% of them wouldn't continue in the program past fall. We also were seeing many scouts dropping out after the first year of camp. So the idea was to develop a program to give them a head start into the scout skills, and hopefully increase our retention both in the troop and at scout camp. The First Class Emphasis was coming out at the same time, trying to get boys to learn their First Class rank within the first year. There was no way to do it all at camp, but we could at least teach them the basic skills and then have their own troop leadership test them, and pass them on the requirements.

My first year at camp was 1974. I took Astronomy Merit Badge, was taught how to swim by Gary "Baron" Watson and Gary Valentine, but otherwise spent most of my time just hiking the trails and hanging out. After I started on staff I kept thinking back to my first year, and thought that it could have been more productive.

When I worked at Bear Lake Scout Camp in 1983 I was involved in running the Natomi program developed a few years earlier by Greg Watson. I thought the idea of a first year program was a good idea. I also was minimally involved in the first year program at Canyon Camp in Illinois. But I thought that they spent too much time on stuff like candle making. So I started with the First Class requirements and tried to figure out how we were going to teach the skills to the Scouts in just one week, really only 5 days.

When I got transferred from Blackhawk Area Council to Lake Huron Area Council in September 1989 and was given the assignment to be the Assistant Camp Director/Program Director at Camp Rotary, I thought that I'd try to initiate the program that I'd been working on for the past several years.

I sat down with Marv in December of 1989 and told him my idea for the program. He liked what he heard, and gave me the go ahead. So over the next month I put everything down on paper. Marv hired Dan Chalk from Midland to be the director of the as of yet unnamed area. I suggested Arik Metevia from my old troop in Bay City to be his assistant. Both of them knew the Scout program well. They knew the skills, and were good instructors. So from about February to June we met frequently to knock out all the details.

We had no idea how the troop leaders would receive it but we planned for a full troop of eight 8-boy-patrols. We decided to use the patrol method in all the teaching. They would start Monday morning by being put into patrols, natural patrols from their home troop when possible and filled out when practical. They went up to Handicraft to make patrol flags, and they came up with patrol names, calls, yells and leadership.

They earned Totin' Chip and Fireman Chit at SCSC, did an edible wild plant nature hike in Nature, spent an afternoon at the Field Sports ranges, learned map and compass, went swimming and learned other basic skills like first aid in the program area.

The name for the area I came up with was Scout-P.A.T.H., which stood for Scout Primary Ability Training Huddle. The metaphor had to do with the Scouting trail or path that they were starting on. I hear other acronyms have developed over the years as well.

Dan and Arik were excellent in helping to make my ideas on a page come to life. They were tested early, because the troop leaders loved the idea. That first year we had several weeks when we had more than 100 scouts in the program. We had to break up into 2 troops with 8 patrols each. We used the old Wood Badge area, which is now the Scout-P.A.T.H. Area and also the clearing behind the Health Lodge where an old campsite once was.

Dan and Arik and I met several times a week to evaluate and improve the program. I tried to be as hands-off as possible because they were the ones that were making it happen. Early on, we came up with the idea of an overnight campout. The requirement at the time said that a scout must pack his own pack and hike five miles to a campsite. Camp isn't that big, so we settled on a mile and a half hike to the gravel pit. The first two years the scouts took everything on their back out to the gravel pit. It was quite a sight seeing over a hundred scouts hiking through camp with their bedroll and supplies. They did the cooking requirements for First Class by cooking their own dinners. It was fun, and they learned something while doing.

During the first three years of the program the campout highlight was the campfire. They would do some songs and skits, and then out of the darkness, Sir Robert Baden Powell would come and address them. He would tell them the story of the scout in the fog that helped bring scouting to the USA, and then Lord Powell would challenge them to keep on the scouting path upwards toward First Class and beyond on the trail to Eagle.

I was Baden Powell, and the effect was pretty good. Afterward each scout was awarded the Scout-P.A.T.H. Award, which was a plastic bear claw on a craft strip. Waz' also kept this P.A.T.H. tradition going when he was Program Director and filled in as Baden Powell as well as telling his goose-bump tales to the 1st year campers.

A few years into the program a pavilion was built in the Scout-P.A.T.H. area. It was dedicated to the memory of an old friend of mine, Jim Rumminger, a scoutmaster from Gladwin Troop 679. He was one of my OA Advisors as a youth, and was one of the real sparkplug scouters who made being a staffer pleasurable. I remember one year he called all the staff to a supposedly urgent meeting in staff lounge. The word was that we were really in for it. We had somehow messed up and were about to get yelled at. He got up in front of the group and started laying in to us. Then he got to the punch line. What we really deserved was…ice cream and watermelon…courtesy of the scoutmasters, and arranged by Jim. Unfortunately Jim passed away from a massive heart attack at the age of 42 while working at Dow Chemical in Midland in 1983. It took almost 20 years to use the memorial money collected in his honor. Many projects were suggested over the years, but finally they ended up building the Scout-P.A.T.H. Pavilion. They had a dedication plaque placed on the side of the pavilion with Jim's picture on it. Waz' was a co-worker with Jim at Dow Chemical and was in camp for the dedication. All of Jim's family and many others were in attendance including Allen Fennell, former Superintendent of Schools from Gladwin and the Camp Director in 62'-63'. I'm proud of the program and hope that today it has the same enthusiasm for giving the new Scout a good head start on the way to First Class as well as getting him into every area of camp.

FRIDAY NIGHT CAMPFIRE

Over the years, one of the hallmark things about Camp Rotary was the Friday Night Campfire. The "pageant style" campfire program, while not unique to Rotary was certainly unique to Michigan Scout Camps. Many scouts go to camp and end up the week watching and participating in the same old skits that you see at every camporee and troop campfires across the country, but not at Camp Rotary, at least not in its heyday. The staff prepared a real stage show highlighting truisms that scouts, leaders, and parents should take home with them. The campfire theater was always packed with visitors who wanted to see what this year's rendition was. Some of the ones that come to my mind are "A Scouting Carol;" an adaptation of Dickens' Christmas Carol using scouting themes, which highlighted the Scouting way, of the past, the present, and the future. I remember the "Ghost of Scouting Future" was none other than Anna "Banana" Hetherington in, about, 1982. Female Scoutmasters were unheard of then, but I guess our prediction came true. Another one I remember was "Camp of Dreams" from 1980. The one I wish I could remember was the one from 1978. I remember it had a great environmental theme. I remember the giant cigarette butt, but I was on the OA ceremony team, so I only saw it from out on the lake.

WATERBACK-WATERFRONT-AQUATICS AREA

One of the greatest natural features of camp is the lake known as Lake Beebe, although the name was legally changed back in 1941 to Rotary Lake. Before we get to the program area, let's relate a little about the lake.

Beebe Lake likely got its name from surveyors who plotted area maps in the 1840's, but may be named after an early settler in the area, Melanchthon Beebe, a Civil War veteran from Vermont. However it got its name, it was well known as a beautiful spot for people to fish, swim and picnic in the 1870's and 1880's. In the winter of 1885, and spring of 1886, the area around Lake Beebe was lumbered. All winter long the logs were piled into the lake in order to send them down the river-system to the mills of Bay City. However, the logs jammed and too much dynamite was used to free them, blowing out the east end of the lake, and dropping its level over 16 feet. For the next 40 years Lake Beebe was scarred by the lumbering, so much so, that literally no one wanted it.

When the Boy Scouts and the Saginaw Rotary Club found the property in 1924, they knew that they needed to raise the lake in order for it to be of any use, so they built an earthen and timber dam that raised the level of the lake 4 feet. This dam lasted only 13 years and was replaced by the current dam in 1937. The new dam raised the level of the lake another 5 feet, restoring nearly 50% of the original lake level.

In the early years, the swimming area was surrounded by a floating dock. Beyond the swimming area were tower rafts that the scouts would dive off of. The beach area was created by importing beach sand, and building a breaker wall to hold back the parade field eroding into the swimming area. The original was built in 1924 or 1925 with improvements and additions being done in the 1940's and the 1980's. The aquatics watchtower has been in the same location since, at least 1936, and is a distinctive landmark of camp. It's been painted different colors throughout the years and the roof and deck have been replaced several times, but it has been the same structure now for about 80 years.

Canoes and rowboats have plied the lake for years but other water craft have as well. In the 1940's, and 1950's prams, small sailboats, were available for scout use. In the 1980's and 1990's large troop rafts were on loan from the National Guard thanks to Ron Comtois, Guardsman, and scoutmaster from Bay City.

After Bear Lake Scout Camp closed in 1985 the small "Catyak" sailboats were brought to Rotary. Unfortunately they were just piled up to rot by the shop. When I came back to camp as Program Director and Assistant Camp Director in 1990, I got the Catyaks working again, extended the boating area, and began our modern sail program. Other sailboats have been purchased, and donated since that time so that many scouts have now sailed the beautiful waters of Lake Beebe.

In the old days even scouts and scouters weren't as environmentally sensitive as we claim to be today. One of the ways that they used to get rid of large unwanted items was to take them out onto the frozen lake during the winter, so that when the spring thaw came, they would just disappear into the lake; out of sight, out of mind. There are probably many items down there, but some that I've seen include a Model T Ford pickup truck and an old safe. The lake bottom is over 70-feet deep in places, so who knows what else may be down there. In the 1970's an underwater nature trail was developed by the staff which began in the beginner's area of the swimming area, and extended along the lake shore to the campfire bowl.

Scouts used snorkels to engage the trail. The lake was a motor-free lake up until 1980 when someone donated an old gas boat motor that was put into the back of one of the aluminum row boats. It was supposed to be a rescue boat but of course it soon became the play-toy of the aquatics staff. Motor boating Merit Badge was also offered beginning in 1981. Now there are several motors on the lake. My own preference would have been to keep the lake motor-free.

The waterfront cabin was donated by Kenneth Guiett and Robert D. Trayer, two scouters from Clare in 1971, and was built by them with help from the scouts of the Clare Troop. It replaced an earlier cabin that was built in about 1940. This newer cabin has served for many years as the summer home of the aquatics staff. In the mid 2000's the back half of the cabin was converted into an equipment locker with the front half remaining a program office for the staff. The porch has served as a lookout point for boating, as well as a great place to just watch the world go by.

One of the fun things that have been talked about for a long time at camp is the name of the area. In the early days it was called either the Aquatics area or the Waterfront. In 1971, Area Director Tom Wills, renamed it the "Water Liberation Front" and then in 1973 Gary Valentine and Rick Berry changed the name to the "Waterback". The story goes that the Waterfront was on the other side of the lake (Fort Scott), and that this made the current aquatics area the Waterback. Initially Marv hated the name, but eventually he was won over and the name stuck. The name lasted until 2000 when the new Camp Director renamed it the Waterfront.

For years the capstone of the week of summer camp was the Saturday morning water carnival. While scoutmasters were up checking out of their campsites, scouts were engaged in canoe swamps, canoe tug-of-wars, canoe in-and-out races, swim relays, gold digging, and of course the watermelon scramble.

There were daily free swims in both afternoon and evening, water polo as a camp-wide activity (East camp vs. West camp). In the early 90's, we arranged the schedule so that there was open boating from after breakfast until 9 P.M. with breaks for lunch and supper. Merit badge classes got first dibs on the watercraft they needed, but the rest were available for use by scouts and scoutmasters alike. Early morning fishing has been a staple for many years, and polar bear swims at 7 A.M. on Tuesdays through Fridays ruled!

Camp Rotary is blessed with one of the finest lakes of any scout camp in America (and probably the world), and it will be the focus of scouting fun in the summer sun for years to come.

FIELD SPORTS

Banging and twanging! What scout doesn't enjoy the opportunity to test his skill with a .22 rifle and a bow and arrow? The current rifle range has been in the same location since 1950. I'm told by old timers that when the current rifle range was plotted, they discovered that the spot they picked, was an old Indian burial mound. Today all work would have stopped and authorities from the Ojibwa nation would be called to sort things out, but in the early 50's, the excavators just worked faster. I can't say for certain that these stories are true, but they have a ring of truth in them.

The blockhouse at the top of the hill, above the rifle range, is a gift of the Alma, Shepherd and Mt. Pleasant Rotary Clubs, donated and constructed in 1965 or 1968 depending on which plaque on the building you can believe. A hand stamped plaque on the door attributes the gift of the building to the Mt. Pleasant Rotary Club in 1965; while a brass plaque on the side of the building says that it was donated by all three clubs in 1968.

In 2007 new archery, rifle, and shotgun pavilions were constructed. They replace the 1950's era construction of Archery and Rifle.

ANDERSON CHAPEL

A Scout is Reverent. This has been not only a point of the Scout Law but also a longstanding practice of Camp Rotary. In the early days chapel services were held on the north side of the lake. Just east of Fort Scott there is a natural bowl, which is now quite grown-over with trees, but at one time was the site of these services. Even before the Boy Scouts came to Lake Beebe, this area was a gathering site for religious services. Perhaps Native Americans came to the lake for their religious ceremonies, but it is documented that Christian revival services, and camp services were held in the oak groves of Fort Scott overlooking the lake in the last decades of the 1800's, and early decades of the 1900's.

In the 1940's a makeshift chapel was constructed near the current site of the Anderson Chapel. In 1956 Frank Andersen, a Saginaw Rotarian and Executive Board member of the Valley Trails Council donated money to build an "A" framed chapel. Originally it had a white cross with a super-imposed yellow Star of David suspended above the altar; this was removed in the early 2000's. In 1974 Anderson donated money to renovate the chapel, adding a chaplain's quarters on the left side of the structure. The right side was for storage of the benches. Over time the structure rotted away and was replaced with a brand new structure in 2006, also a gift from the Anderson Foundation.

CARNEY HEALTH LODGE

Dr. Thomas Carney was a physician from Alma who was also a Rotarian, and member of the Valley Trails Council Executive Board. He served as the non-resident physician for summer camp for a number of years. When he died at the age of 80 in 1949, he willed money for the construction of a health lodge at camp. Construction and dedication took place in 1952. The structure included a medical check in office, an isolation sick room and living quarters. When Marv Valentine was hired as the first onsite Ranger in 1970, he and his family lived in the health lodge during that first year until the Ranger's Residence, (now the Camp Director's Residence) was built. From 1952 through the early 2000's it was the ritual, of every scout and scouter who came to camp, to come through the health lodge during Sunday check in for their health checks. They then received their buddy tag to take down to the aquatics area for their swim check. This procedure was changed in 2007. There was a feeling from the camp administration that the health lodge was too small, and a bottleneck in the check-in process. So later, health checks were done on the bottom floor of Central Lodge, and then still later there were multiple health stations set up on the parade field outside the commissioner's and steward's cabins. The health lodge has also been used for year-round staff housing. During the 1970's-1990's camp participated in Central Michigan University's Recreation

Department's internship program. Student interns would live, and work at camp for a period of time working either on summer staff or year-round in the Outdoor Education Program. They also helped with camp maintenance and weekend program. When this program wasn't used any longer, a Camp Master program was started. Volunteer leaders were recruited and trained to provide weekend support to the camp. They checked in troops, and other groups using the camp facilities, offered different program features, and gave the Camp Ranger relief, and actual time off on weekends. Harold Schmidt from Saginaw was the first director of the Camp Master Program which was in place from 1989-2000. Camp Masters stayed in the health lodge. Mike Bingham, a regular participant in the program, remodeled the health lodge for the Camp Masters use in the 1990's.

RAPPELLING AND PROJECT COPE

Rappelling first came to Camp Rotary in the summer of 1975 when John Ramey a former paratrooper was hired to be Provisional Scoutmaster. Initially the camp water tower, built in 1960, but later abandoned, became the location for rappelling. The first year, two styles of rappelling were offered, first the traditional style that is still used, of jumping backwards from the top station bouncing off of the side of the structure down to the ground. The second method was called Australian Style. This method was the same as the first accept that you went down face first rather than backwards. Participants had to climb up a small medal ladder to access the catwalk around the base of the water holding tank. The instructor had to tie himself off to the steel barrel rings of the tank so as not to be pulled off of the tower by nervous participants. I was almost pulled off more than once, including once by a 350 lbs. scout leader who was so scared that he tried to climb back into the tower after dangling over the edge for several minutes.

In 1981, the water tank was removed from the superstructure and a new platform and launching station built on the top of the tower. This platform was much safer and offered some better seasonal protection for the participants.

There was a desire by Marv Valentine to build a whole new rappelling tower that included climbing faces as well. For a number of years in the

1970's and 1980's, Marv went around the state looking at other ropes courses and climbing/rappelling towers to get ideas for our project. He also collected old utility poles that were gathered from around the state. This was in the planning stages for about 15 years with not much progress towards actual construction until 1991 when I was able to bring all the right people together to make it happened. Bill Marshall was my District Chairman for White Birch District, (I was District Executive at the time) which included Clare, Isabella and Gratiot Counties. Bill was Vice President of Mears Engineering in Rosebush, which was an oilfield pipeline contractor. Bill had access to the equipment to set the poles for the course and tower. Don Thayer from Clare was my District commissioner. Don had all sorts of heavy equipment which he used to shape the course, remove trees, etc. Frank Gerace owned a construction company in Midland and was on the Lake Huron Area Council Executive Board. He agreed to be general contractor for the building of the tower and course. This was his first project in camp, along with the replacement of the footbridge going towards Pike Lodge. Over the fall and spring of 1991-92, the tower and course were built. While Frank's crews did the big parts of the project, much of the work was done by Frank, Don, Marv, and I. The new program area went into use in the summer of 1992. The area consisted of the rappelling/climbing tower which featured three progressive climbing surfaces as well as the rappelling face, an all-season launching station at the top, an equipment locker inside the tower, three "chimney" climbs inside the tower, and finally a winding staircase inside the tower which led to the top launching station. Greg Wasmer and Don Thayer were sent off to National Camp School and were Rotary's first certified C.O.P.E instructors.

A second phase of the C.O.P.E. area was never fully completed. The idea was that the C.O.P.E. course would be marketed to various outside groups: police departments, college classes, business groups, etc. but the drawback to making this marketing effective was where to house the participants. While dormitory style cabins work for scout groups, these other outside organizations are less likely to enjoy this arrangement. So while some of these groups have indeed used the course from time to time, they tend to be day-use only. The idea was to construct 12 to15 two to four man cabins on the western portions of what is now Curtis campsite. These cabins would be accessible by car from the maintenance area. During the summer, these would be staff cabins, and during the off season they would be rented to C.O.P.E. participants and the like. In 1998 and 1999 these cabins were indeed built. But unfortunately there was disagreement about where to put them. The big picture was the multiple usages of the cabins; however the smaller picture was to just build them in the area that had been "staff camp" for years. The second approach prevailed; except that they were built as being "moveable." They are on skids and are just "pigtailed" into the utilities so that they can be moved to a new location at any time.

They of course have never been moved, and they are currently unavailable for rent. The C.O.P.E. course and Climbing/Rappelling Tower could have been used more to their fullest potential.

As a side note, when the high course was built in 1991-92, it was built 55 to 60 foot off the ground. The last event was a "slide for life" that jettisoned over a valley lined with pine trees. The affect was stimulating. In 2002 or 2003, a gentleman that owned a company that marketed special pole for C.O.P.E. courses, joined the national committee on C.O.P.E. He was able to get the standard changed on what kind of poles was allowable for B.S.A. C.O.PE courses. Interestingly enough, the only acceptable poles under the new guidelines were the ones exclusively marketed by his company. While many camps around the country protested these new guide lines, our camp decided to follow them. The high course was chain sawed to the ground. New poles were purchased and installed (at great expense, mostly supplied by the Mischigonong Lodge.) These poles were much shorter than the original course, topping out at 35 foot rather and 55. Within 6 months of the building of the new high course, the gentleman left the national committee and the standard was dismissed.

HANDICRAFT

Handicrafts have been part of summer camping since there has been summer camping, even before it became a part of a B.S.A. activity. At Camp Rotary there is a long history of the area going all the way back to the days before the scouts came to Lake Beebe. Some of the highlights I have come to know, include the knowledge that in the mid 1930's, a very popular Handicraft Director at camp was Ira "Cy" Butterfield. "Cy" was a student at the U. of M. and hailed from Bay City, and was the first Eagle Scout from Bay County. He ran a very dynamic program that kept Scouts wanting to come back to camp to engage in his handicrafts. Butterfield later went on to become a very popular District Judge in Bay City, and a noted historian. His personal papers make up a large historical collection of scouting history at the Clarke Historical Library at CMU.

In the late 1950's, Handicraft Director Ted Scheall, who eventually became a Camp Director, created two totem poles in the handicraft area. They originally were part of the camp entrance on old US-27. Today they are located outside the camp office, and at the Valentine Campfire Amphitheater.

The location of the Handicraft Area has moved around several times during our history. Early on it was located in both the old, and the new Deer Lodge. The new Deer Lodge was built in 1958 as a donation from Saginaw Rotarian Perry Shorts, who also donated the football stadium at CMU. It housed not only the Handicraft Area, but also served as the Trading Post during the summer camp season. When the new Trading Post was built in 1979 on the footprint of the old mess hall, the Handicraft Area followed it to the OA room, and the Trading Post pavilion area. The sound of banging mallets for leather craft was overwhelming at times, and so for a few summers it was housed in the old Camp Office (now known as Raccoon Lodge). About the year 2000, it returned to Deer Lodge.

HIGH ADVENTURE – OLDER BOY PROGRAM

There has always been a challenge to get scouts to come back to camp beyond their 3rd year. Most scouts, when they start to hit high school stop coming to camp in favor of summer jobs, girls and cars (not necessarily in that order). Back in the late 1940's, and early 1950's, plans were put into effect to develop programs with the older Scout in mind. In 1951, a new area was opened on the north side of the lake for Explorer Scouts. Back in the day, explorers were scouts 14 years old and above. An Explorer Advisor from Caro was hired to be the Explorer Program Director. His name was Emerson Scott. Scott was world famous for his 5,000 mile canoe trek in 1950, from Ojibway Island in Saginaw to the Arctic Circle. In honor of their leader, the Explorers named the new area "Fort Scott."

In the 1970's the Pioneer Camp Program was developed. It took Scouts out to North Camp to build a log cabin. They learned Dutch oven cooking, earned Pioneering and Cooking Merit Badges, and had a god ole time of it.

In 1981, a Voyager program was developed. This was a 5-day canoe trip that put in at Reedsburg Dam on the Muskegon River, just west of Houghton Lake, and took out at Evart, Michigan. In the spring of 1981, Rick Berry, and I plotted the course. We canoed the river, found camping sites along the way, made arrangements with some private property owners for camping rights, and figured how far the trekkers could get in 5-days on the river. It became a fairly popular program. A Voyager staff person was hired by the camp to be the program guide. Scouts needed to be 14 years old and at least 1st Class, have the approval of their scout leader, and have at least one other adult go on the trip. The program was offered for about 15 summers until the canoe trailers became so worn out that they were scrapped, and so was the program. Since 1997, there hasn't been much in high adventure or specific older boy programs offered.

I have so many wonderful memories over the past 40 years. Just thinking about them brings back the good ole days of summer at the best camp in the whole world...my second home...Camp Rotary.

My brothers Tom and George and I during our
first stay at Camp Rotary—1972

CHAPTER 2

THE HISTORY OF MISCHIGONONG LODGE #89

By: Erv Hutter

Mischigonong Lodge #89 was formed in 1971 upon the creation of the new Lake Huron Area Council, 265. The lodge was comprised of three former lodges--the Tittabawasink Lodge #469 of the Paul Bunyan Council, the Kepayshowink Lodge # 89 of the Saginaw Bay Area Council (Previously the Summer Trails Council of Bay City and the Valley Trails Council of Saginaw) --and the eastern part of the Indian Drum Lodge # 152 of the Scenic Trails Council (Traverse City). Even prior to the adoption of the OA as a national BSA program, there were other camp honor societies in our council area.

The Order of the Arrow was founded in 1915 at Treasure Island Scout Camp, Philadelphia (PA) Council, by its Camp Director, E. Urner

Goodman and Assistant Camp Director Carroll A. Edson. It was created as an honor camper society to recognize those scouts who best exemplified the living of the precepts of the Scout Oath and Law while at summer camp. Several other honor camper societies sprang up at other scout camps, and these quickly spread from camp to camp around the country. In this area, the *Tribe of Gimogash* existed in the Summer Trails Council at Camp Haley and Camp Neyati from about 1931 to 1942. It was brought here by Camp Director and Scout Executive "Chief" George Landane.

In 1934 the Boy Scouts of America officially recognized the Order of the Arrow as an approved society within the Scouting Movement (although it wasn't fully integrated until 1948). In 1936, the program came to Valley Trails Council at Camp Kepayshowink (Camp Rotary) started by Camp Director and Scout Executive J. Herbert Saum. However these organizations were always camp based, and as Camp Directors changed the program, was sometimes discontinued. The Kepayshowink Lodge, while first started in 1936, stopped functioning after a few years and was reinstated in 1942 by Camp Director E.B. Clark. The same year, Chief Landane merged his Gimogash program into the approved Order of the Arrow program, keeping the name Gimogash for the new Lodge.

Summer Trails Council was formed in 1927 by the merging of the Bay City Council (1917) and the Midland Council (1919). It was made up of the following counties: Bay, Huron, Tuscola (part), Midland, Gladwin, Arenac, Iosco, Roscommon, and Ogemaw. Alcona, Oscoda, Crawford, Alpena, Montmorency, Otsego, Presque Isle, and Cheboygan. Its summer camps were Camp Haley (1926-1947) near Selkirk, on Henderson Lake, Camp Neyati (1937-1962) near Lake Station, on Crooked Lake, and Bear Lake Scout Camp (1954-1985) near Kalkaska on Bear Lake. The Council was headquartered in Bay City.

Valley Trails Council was founded in 1928 in Saginaw. Previously the Saginaw Council had existed from 1918 to 1928. VTC was made up of the following counties: Saginaw, Gratiot, Isabella, Clare and part of Tuscola. Its summer camp was Camp Rotary (1926-present), sometimes called Camp Kepayshowink, near Clare. It was headquartered in Saginaw.

In 1947 the northern counties of Alcona, Oscoda, Crawford, Alpena, Montmorency, Otsego, Presque Isle, and Cheboygan became part of Scenic Trails Council, headquartered in Traverse City.

In 1951, Midland, Gladwin, Arenac, Roscommon and Ogemaw, counties formed the new Paul Bunyan Council, headquartered in Midland. Camp Neyati (1937-1962) was its summer camp until the opening of Paul Bunyan Scout Reservation in 1963.

In 1961, when Valley Trails and Summer Trails Councils merged to form Saginaw Bay Area Council, the two lodges merged, keeping the name and number of Kepayshowink #89. Scouts camped at Rotary and Bear Lake.

In 1971, Saginaw Bay Area Council merged with Paul Bunyan Council, and the eastern portion of Scenic Trails Council. It comprises 19 counties including: Bay, Huron, Tuscola, Saginaw, Gratiot, Isabella, Clare, Midland, Gladwin, Arenac, Iosco, Ogemaw, Roscommon, Alcona, Oscoda, Montmorency, Presque Isle, Otsego, and Crawford. It is headquartered near Auburn, Michigan. Its summer camps include Camp Rotary (1926-present), Bear Lake Scout Camp (1954-1985) and Paul Bunyan Scout Reservation (1963-present).

With the creation of the new Lake Huron Area Council, a new lodge was formed. Mischigonong, kept the lodge number of Kepayshowink #89, but renamed itself. Mischigonong's charter members chose the canoe as the lodge symbol or totem, and designed the first lodge flap--three canoes with W.W.W. superimposed on them. The name "Mischigonong" comes from the Ottawa Indians, and means, "Land of the Great Lakes." (Al Barnes' book *Supper in the Evening* describes the Ottawas and their use of the word "Mischigonong" to characterize the land about them.) Even earlier, Fr. Jacques Marquette inscribed the word "Mischigonong" on his map in reference to the lake we now call Lake Michigan. He ascribes the name to the Miami people's nomenclature.

The lodge originally consisted of ten chapters, but today is organized into six. Each one of the council's districts is an Order of the Arrow Chapter. These are: Shoreline District, TOBICO Chapter; Ojibway District, KEPAYSHOWINK Chapter; Thumb District, NISWI ISHKODEN Chapter; Tall Pine District, KWENI-KUWE Chapter; Chippewa District, CHIPPEWA Chapter; and Thunderhead District, NEGWEGON Chapter.

During the Lodge's 40-year history, Mischigonong has been awarded the national E. Urner Goodman Camping Award in 1980, 2009, and

2011and the section DeCourcy Award in 1976 and 1994, 2008, 2009, 2011, and 2012. Both of these awards are for achievement in camping promotions. More recently, the lodge received a $2,500 matching grant for the "Year In Service" program by the National Order of the Arrow Committee. This money was matched by the lodge and the total $5,000 was used to develop a handicapped accessible site at Camp Rotary. In 1986, the lodge hosted over 3,600 Arrowmen from around the nation at Central Michigan University for the National Order of the Arrow Conference (NOAC) entitled "Kindle the Flame from Within."

The lodge has elected 34 youth to serve as its chief. They include:

1. Pat Beck — 1971-1972 and 1972-1973
2. Dave Wagner — 1973-1974
3. Paul Blanchard — 1974-1975
4. Craig Bowen — 1975-1976
5. Brian Brophey — 1976-1977
6. Dale Foster — 1977-1978
7. Greg Watson — 1978-1979
8. Erv Hutter — 1979-1980
9. Robert Foltz — 1980-1981
10. Tom Stoppa — 1981-1982
11. Bob Nicol — 1982-1983
12. Mark Blanchard — 1983-1984
13. Kent Holsing — 1984-1985
14. Tim Brooks — 1985-1986
15. Jeff Schultz — 1986-1987
16. Bob Rhode — 1987-1988
17. Steve Townsend — 1988-1989
18. Dave Ryder — 1989-1990
19. Dave Sheppard — 1990-1991
20. Derek Kimball — 1991-1992 and 1992-1993
21. Tom Olver — 1993-1994
22. Marc Orth — 1994-1995
23. Ted Kremer — 1995-1996
24. Tom White — 1996-1997
25. Eric Gorney — 1997-1998

26.	Chris Van Arsdale	1998-1999
27.	Aaron Gorney	1999-2000
28.	Adam Dutkiewicz	2000-2001
29.	Mark Van Arsdale	2001-2002
30.	Chris Tack	2002-2003 and 2003-2004
31.	Eric Curtis	2004-2005 and 2005-2006
32.	Matthew VanArsdale	2006-2007
33.	Storm Shriver	2007 – 2008
34.	Justin Biver	2008–2009 and 2009– 2010
35.	Kyle Borchard	2010 – 2011
36.	Kevin Schoenknecht	2011 – 2012

Three Arrowmen, Brian Brophey, 1978; Brian Yoder, 1982; and Ken Ruppel, 1989; have been elected Section Chief from our lodge. Others have served as section officers.

The Council Scout Executives have appointed ten adults Lodge Advisor over the past 40 years. These Arrowmen are:

1.	Roy Chase	1971-1973
2.	Roger Sucharski	1973-1976
3.	Robert Donaghue	1976-1981
4.	John Foltz	1981-1986
5.	Doug Catlin	1986-1988
6.	Marcus Haubenstricker	1988-1992
7.	George Strom	1992-1996
8.	Ken Kueffner	1996-2005
9.	Frank Welling	2005- 2006
10.	Tom Stoppa	2006 -2012

Over the years, the Mischigonong Lodge of the Order of the Arrow has donated significant monies toward camp promotions and physical improvements of our council camps. Besides many of the small priced improvements, a few of the big-ticket items have been $5,000 for the COPE program at Camp Rotary and $1,500 for the rail fencing at Paul Bunyan. In 1997, the sum of $7,500 was allocated for several long-term projects at Paul Bunyan including repairs and reconstruction of the rifle range shelter, and parade ground improvements. Likewise, the lodge has donated a yearly amount so that underprivileged scouts may attend summer camp and has given countless hours of physical labor towards the improvement and upkeep of Paul Bunyan and Rotary. In 2007, the lodge developed a plan to designate the $5,000 yearly money earned from the sale of the Light House patches. Such categories include: Fellowship Projects; Camperships: Long-Term; and National Events / Training. Beginning in 2008, the lodge, too, presented to the council a $1,000.00 James E. West donation in honor of an individual. For 2010, the 100 Anniversary of Scouting, the lodge plans to donate $5,000.00 and apply for an additional $5,000 through the National Lodges Serve Grant fund. The money will be used towards building YURTS at Paul Bunyan Scout Reservation.

Each year, Mischigonong Lodge presents the Founder's Award, which is a national award given on the lodge level to no more than two members (one youth and one adult) who have given outstanding service to the lodge and demonstrate the ideals of the Order described by our founder. Past recipients are:

Richard Thompson (1982)
Tom Stoppa and Robert Donaghue (1984)
Bob Nicol and George Strom (1985)
Mark Blanchard and Richard "Waz" Wasmer (1986)
Ken Ruppel and Jack Beamish (1987)
Jeff Schultz and D. Hugh Clark (1988)
Brian Mowry and Thomas Jane (1989)
Dave Sheppard and James Mowry (1990)
Charlie Looker and John Foltz (1991)
Clinton Andrews and Noel Ryder (1992)
George Doak and Dan Beard (1994)
Peter Starland and Marcus Haubenstricker (1995)
Mark Orth and Mary Lou Jones (1996)
Ted Kremer and John England (1997)
Chris Van Arsdale and Michael Smith (1998)
Eric Gorney and Ken Kueffner (1999)
Eric French and Larry Smith (2000)

Guy Payne and Don Schultz (2001)
Chris Fehrman and Bob Jones (2002)
Doug Merriam and Clyde French (2003)
Mark Van Arsdale and Don Pashby (2004)
Eric Curtis and Herb Voltz (2005)
Matthew Van Arsdale (2006)
Brandon Armstrong and Chris Tack (2007)
Jeff Schubring, Jr. and Jim Murphy (2008)
Sam Hadden and Steve Tack (2009)
Logan Harvey and Mike Herrington (2010)
Brad Koch and Jeanne Armstrong (2011)
Kevin Schoenknecht and John Ruppel (2012)

In 2007 the lodge had an active membership roster of 550, inducting approximately 80 Ordeal Members, and 35 Brotherhood Members at our Fellowships. Nearly 48 Arrowmen traveled to Rota-Kiwan near Kalamazoo to participate in the annual Section 2B Conclave. The lodge sent five representatives to the 2007 National Order of the Arrow Summit. These included Matthew Van Arsdale, Lodge Chief; Storm Shriver, Vice Chief of Membership; Justin Biver, Vice Chief of Finances, Mike Herrington, Staff Adviser; and Tom Stoppa, Lodge Adviser. Mr. Mike Parmer and Mr. Jeff Stevens served on the summit medical staff.

In the 2008 year, the lodge's membership is at 400 inducting almost 85 new members and sealing the membership of 50 Brotherhood members. A new "pre-paid" brotherhood system was adopted and over $5,000 donated to the council camping programs for fellowship supplies, camperships, promotions items, and youth training. Almost 40 Arrowmen traversed to Traverse City and Camp Greilick, home of the Drum, for the 2008 conclave. At the conclave, Logan Harvey was elected Section Vice-Chief and the lodge received the DeCourcy Camping Award for its efforts towards camp promotions in the 2007 year. In the summer, five members trekked to Wyoming to join over 1,000 other Arrowmen from around the nation for ArrowCorps5. Spending a week in the Tetons trailing building and/or serving on the medical staff were: Logan Harvey, Mike Herrington, Tom Stoppa, Jeff Stevens, and Mike Parmer. At the annual fall fellowship, Justin Biver was elected Lodge Chief.

In 2009, membership barely grew to 401 Arrowmen, but the lodge earned the Quality Lodge Award for the 2008 year and converted over 35% of the Ordeal membership to Brotherhood. At the section conclave, the lodge received the DeCourcy Award for the second year in a row. Over the course of the year, the lodge once again contributed over $5,000 to the council and instituted recognition through the council's James E. West Endowment Fund. In the spring, the Van Arsdale family, John, Carol, Christopher, Mark, and Matthew, were the lodge first recipients of the lodge's James E. West award. By mid-summer, the lodge approved $5,000.00 towards the PBSR Yurt project and planned to apply for a matching grant through the National OA Service Award. At the end of July, 25 members traveled to Bloomington, IN to celebrate the 94 anniversary of the Order at the National Order of the Arrow Conference themed: *The Power of One*. In the fall of the year, the lodge held one of its largest inductions for 91 Ordeal Arrowmen. Plans were being readied to assist the council in celebrating Scouting's 100 year.

For the Centennial Year 2010, the lodge tackled many projects including:

- National Service Grant – receiving $2,500 from the national Order of the Arrow lodge
- Hosting the C2B Conclave at Camp Rotary – with 81 lodge members celebrating Goodman's "Technicolor Dream"
- Developing a Service Turtle Pin - that could only be earned by working on a 2010 program
- Holding two fellowship – as usual and inducting over 75 new Ordeals and 40 Brotherhood members
- Assisting at the Centennial Encampment – held in Alpena at the CRTC attended by 1400 scouts and scouters
- Building YURTs at PBSR – and donating $5,000 towards this projects, too!
- Leading the council in its' service program – Project SaginAWESOME – with 140 Arrowmen contributing over 1100 hours in partnership with Saginaw's Habitat for Humanity.

More Arrowmen gave more financial contributions, more time, and more talent in recognition of Scouting's 100th Year. In 2010, the membership grew to 410 as the lodge continued to earn the National Quality Lodge Award. In this same year, Mischigonong learned they had earned and received the E. Urner Goodman Camping Award for their efforts in 2009. These efforts included: donation of supplies to both camps, hosting two work weekend fellowships, promoting troop camping, providing adult provisional leadership to boys who cannot attend camp with their unit, and creating a 1st year Camper Patch. The lodge donated over $10,000 and continued to recognize quality Arrowmen with the James E. West Award presenting it to Herb Volz at the June 2010 Council Dinner.

By 2011, the lodge maintained its high standards and continued its successes with:

- Receiving the National Quality Lodge Award
- Earning the National Service Award (for the first time in its history)
- Winning the section camping award – the DeCourcy – for the third time in four years!
- Receiving the E. Urner Goodman Camping Award

Membership continued to grow with an additional Arrowmen. The lodge's Brotherhood conversion stood at nearly 50% because of its implementation of the pre-paid Brotherhood program. Financial support and service hours continued to be a focus of the program with over $7,000.00 donated back to the Lake Huron Area Council and its camping properties.

In the spring of 2011, the lodge also received a $25,000.00 service grant from Dow Chemical to partner with Habitat for Humanity the local Veterans hospital, and the Deindorfer Woods park association to revitalize the park in Saginaw. Mr. Brad Koch and Mrs. Carol Van Arsdale lead this project, dubbed SaginAWESOME, once again. The lodge donated $1,000.00 to the James E. West fund and recognized former lodge adviser, Ken Kueffner, with this honor.

During the 2012 year, the Lodge met with representatives from three other lodges in Michigan to combine efforts, enact the Michigan

Program, and create a new lodge. The Mischigonong representatives were Kevin Schoenknecht, Jake Straub, Craig Symborksi, Michael Wright, Ken Kueffner, and Tom Stoppa. On August 4, 2012 – the last day of the 2012 National Order of the Arrow Conference, Agaming Maangowgwan 804 came into existence from the legacy lodges of Chickagami, Cuwe, GabeShi-Win-Gi-Ji-Kens, & Mischigonong.

(Author's acknowledgment: Scouter Tom Stoppa, OA Keeper of the Records contributed to the preceding lodge History).

CHAPTER 3

CAMP ROTARY TODAY

By Andrew Wright

With the turn of the new millennium came many new changes for Camp Rotary. The biggest of these was a new Camp Director. With Marv Valentine retiring after 30 years of service to camp, Edward Hoolehan stepped up as the new Director. Ed had some big plans for the camp, many of which took place almost immediately. Although some of these changes were not greeted very well, they have become an integral part of Camp Rotary.

Many changes took place in camp infrastructure. An addition was put onto the front of the Camp Director's residence, making the house more spacious and easier to live in. The loft in the Camp Office was enclosed and became the Directors Office. A new porch and ramp were donated and constructed by a troop for the front of the office. The obstacle course behind SCSC was turned into a walking trail. The camp colors were changed from "camp brown" to "elk tan" and "alpine view green."

Other projects that happened under Ed's tenure were:

- The remodel of Deer Lodge to include a new look for camp, half-log siding.
- The remodel of the old Camp Office, Raccoon Lodge into Weekend Ranger housing.

- The addition of a deck off the north side of the Dining Hall
- The re-design and building of the Nature Trail (designed, laid-out and built by Ryan McCullough, Troop 48, Marion, MI.)
- The building of the Ted Doan Conference Center to include the Camp Rotary Court of Honor Brick Walk – located on the back porch.
- The re-design of the Valentine Amphitheater Fire bowl performance area
- The removal of the railroad tie steps from most hillside walking trails – which were later smoothed and covered with pea gravel to prevent erosion.
- The creation of the Camp Rotary Clare witch Project – a haunted hayride through camp used as a fundraiser.

Another change was the renaming of the aquatics area. Always known as the Waterback, this area was now referred to as the Waterfront. Ed also introduced the "Spirit of the Eagle" ceremony at the closing campfires to honor all Eagle Scouts in attendance, especially those who Camp Rotary had helped in attaining their Eagle rank. It was these changes and others that helped in moving Camp Rotary forward.

In 2007, Ed served his last summer as Camp Director and then retired. His successor was former District Executive and Camp Director of Paul Bunyan Scout Reservation, Brad Murray. Brad continued to improve both P.B.S.R. and Rotary's infrastructure and their programs.

Brad officially started at camp in January of 2008 where he immediately began to grow our off-season clientele list. Currently, Rotary offers off-season programs to football camps, church camps, business retreats, school retreats, scout troops, band camps, cheerleader camps and many others. This off-season programming along with our dynamic summer program has helped keep Rotary in the black for many years.

Other projects that have taken place under Brad include:

- The building of a new storage building in the maintenance are
- The removal of the semi-truck storage trailers from the maintenance area.

- The removal of the fireplace from the Central Dining Hall to make more space.
- The remodeling of the old tent room in the basement of the Dining Hall into a functional class room.
- The remodeling of the Camp Office.
- The building of brand new Shooting Sport Ranges.
- The building of numerous new pavilions throughout camp.
- The re-roofing of the Dining Hall to include a steel roof.
- The expansion of seating in the Valentine Amphitheater Fire bowl.

In October of 2014, Brad accepted a promotion and became the Operations Director of Michigan Crossroads Council Outdoor Adventures.

CAMP PROGRAM AND CHANGES THROUGH-OUT THE YEARS

The following will include observations from my three different perspectives; first as a scout then as a staff member and as a Camp Commissioner/Program Director.

My first memories of camp begin in June of 2000, when I attended Camp Rotary as a first-year camper in the P.A.T.H. Program. Here I underwent training in basic Scouting skills. This program has grown throughout the years to accommodate sixty plus scouts a week. It has also withstood the many advancement changes and has had the program adapted to meet these requirements. I spent my first three summers on staff as an instructor there.

Upon becoming a C.I.T., under the Waz', I got more involved in the camp program, especially on the Order of the Arrow side. It was as a C.I.T. that I began to learn exactly what camp was all about. From staff fellowship to merit badge instruction to staff/scout interaction, it became clear that working at camp was like living with a family. It was a non-paying job, but it also had other benefits, like the benefit of a smile you got from another scout's face. It was an opportunity for me to pass on what I've learned to others; so that they also could implement the same knowledge and skills in their lives. Thus began my career at Camp Rotary.

Over the years, there have been many changes to the program. Some of these changes have stuck and are now a part of tradition. Others have run through trial and error phases and are now a part of Camp Rotary's history. These are some of the most notable changes that have taken part at camp since the change of the millennium; first, the removal of the original type obstacle course from behind the SCSC Area. As a scout, I vaguely remember running this obstacle course, but with the memory so faint, it must had been impressive. I say this because other makeshift courses have been built throughout the years in SCSC area, but none have seen the volume or use of the original one. The area has also seen a growth in interest, especially with Camping and Cooking Merit Badges being Eagle required. In addition to the traditional merit badges, we now offer Cycling, Hiking, Archaeology, Geo-coaching and Search and Rescue. This adds new and exciting programs for scouts to take part in. SCSC has also become famous for its evening programs: the 50 knot club, monkey fist tying demonstrations, burn the rope competition, lumberjack challenge and the popular 9-hole putt-putt course.

The next change comes in the opening campfire program. In the past, each program area performed an individual skit in order to introduce their program. This has changed. A good deal of staff week is now spent in planning, writing and performing a 45 minute story line style skit that pertains to the summer's theme. Themes like Camp Rotary at the Summer Olympics, Walking in their Moccasins, Search and Discover Your Future. The original basis for the Sunday night campfire is still shown in this new style of skit, each area still has the opportunity to introduce itself to the camp. With the remodeling of the campfire bowl, skits now also contain music and special effects to give an extra punch. Silly costumes and ending of the campfire with either, "We Are the Staffers of Camp Rotary" (words by Waz' and Dan Tanciar in the 90's) or "Scout Vespers" are still part of the campfire tradition.

Waz' points out that the Wednesday afternoon carnival (started by Waz and Ed Hoolehan) is as much a success today as it was when it started out as an outdoor pig roast back in the early 2000's. Scout Leaders are still being dunked in water. In fact, the original dunk-tank, used back then, is still in use thanks to generosity of a Scoutmaster from Rosebush, Michigan. The carnival is now held on the Parade Field and not on the outside area east of Central Dining Hall. Although it's no longer a pig roast, the camp still eats, outdoors, picnic style with a great summer time flare. Some of the games have changed, there's no longer the "Grease Pole" to climb (although it's still there) and the hole-in-one competition, but there are many other fun things for the scouts to do. The Scout Leaders Chili Cook-Off is held during the carnival.

The Dining Hall. The era of rectangle wooden tables with benches that fall over with a deafening "boom" anytime someone stood up are gone. In the early 2000's the beat up wooden tables were replaced with round tables and chairs. This was done in order to make more room in the dining area. In 2006, an extension was put on the back deck, giving a cool, quiet place with a great view for leader's to get away and relax. This also became the new gathering place for adult leader meetings.

In 2011, a much-needed face-lift was given to the dining hall. The iconic fireplace was removed in order to make room for our growing numbers. The old, tired rubber roof was replaced with metal and extended over the new walk-in-cooler and freezer as well as over the new deck. Along with this project came the addition of a new septic field and dining hall sound system.

With the dining hall now packed at 360-person capacity, we needed to make sure that our dining hall program was still entertaining and memorable like the old days. The iconic Golden Banana Award (now awarded to the loudest, cleanest, most energetic table, not the quietest) still follows every meal as do the skits, songs and shows that are always loved and enjoyed by the campers. It is not uncommon to see Darth Vader, a Ninja turtle, the village People, an up-and-coming rock band and many other gigs during the dining hall experience.

The shooting sports program has also come a long way. Many remember the red rifle pavilion with the rotting roof and makeshift table to hold the clay thrower. And also the small teaching pavilion at the archery range with a shooting line that caused you to bake in the hot summer sun. These are gone and have been replaced with new, state-of-the-art ranges. The rifle and archery ranges both boast a new covered shooting line with teaching area and lockable storage on-site. These new facilities can accommodate a 16 person shooting line and require the use of two instructors. The new shotgun range, separate from the other ranges, is still in its infancy, but is slated to have 5 different shooting stations with multiple trap houses. In addition to merit badges, the ranges host a variety of specialty programs to include: muzzle loading rifle and pistol shoots, action archery, NRA marksman awards, slingshot shooting, tomahawk and knife throwing and the shotgun skills competition.

The Aquatics Area. The t-dock, floating docks and boating dock have all been replaced with a new floating dock system donated by the Saginaw Rotary Club. This system now allows for our docks to be left in on a year-round basis and removes the tedious task of removing the docks from the water each season. The popular program for the Waterfront still exists. Some of the newer aspects to the area include paddleboats, the Iceberg (a 14-foot climbing wall and slide in the middle of the lake), and the new stand-up paddleboards, which allow for both the earning of the BSA Stand-up Paddleboard Award. The BSA Lifeguard Program has been replaced with the new national training referred to as Paddle Craft Safety and Swimming and Water Rescue. A newer take on the old water carnival is the Scoutmaster Belly Flop Contest, the mile swim and snorkeling. New exciting programs include the cannon ball competition, cardboard boat race and the Aquatics Ninja Warrior which is a timed aquatics obstacle course. Still popular when it was added a few years ago is the camp's fishing tournament.

The Nature Area is very much the same with the exception of some upgrades. The Patterson Family (Stew and Stub) donated a much-needed teaching pavilion and a self-guided nature trail was put in. Brad Coulson still serves as the Nature Director, a position he had held for more than 27 years. Besides the exciting older programs, the new additions are the Turtle Toddle Obstacle Course and a Nabbing Nature session teaching scouts how to safely catch turtles, frogs and snakes.

Handicraft Area has had some changes also. All of the traditional merit badges are still offered and the evening programs have become a hit. Scouts can use their imagination and play with Legos, can show off their artistic skills during the art gallery and can tie-dye their own custom shirt to take home. The new Chess Merit badge is also a hit.

COPE and Climbing are still a big part of Rotary's program. The 40-foot climbing tower is always busy with scouts wanting to climb and rappel and the 13-element low course and 5-element high course always fill up. The big attraction to the climbing area, the Night Crawler, started in 2004 and still fills up to day because who doesn't want to climb, rappel and zip-line in the dark with no more than a glow-stick for light.

With growing attendance also comes the need for new programs. In 2009, Rotary saw its first new program area, M.A.D.E. MADE stands for "Multimedia Application Design Environment" (or MADE at Camp Rotary) and serves the new technology area of camp. Here we teach badges such as Communications, Graphic Arts, Photography, Movie Making, Music, Theater, Model Design and Building and others. This area along with its Video Game themed evening programs draws many scouts, especially the older scouts who have already completed many of the traditional summer camp merit badges. While the video game programs may be controversial and if that is what it takes to get a scout to camp to enjoy and be introduced to other aspects that it has to offer, then it is a welcome program.

A second new program area started in the summer of 2013; Industrial Arts. The Industrial Arts area was built off of two things: the donation of equipment from Lincoln electric and the need for new programs for older scouts. Scouts taking part in the program can learn skills such as Farm mechanics, Plumbing, electricity and Welding.

While the programs offer and grow with the times, one thing always stays the same: we never forget the camp motto "Let the Adventure Begin." All of the changes come from the ideas and suggestions of our staff, our program committee and most importantly, our scouts. Camp Rotary will always continue to offer fun and exciting programs so that Scouts can create their own memorable adventure.

SUMMER CAMP STAFF

Being a Rotary Staffer is a challenging and rewarding job. We definitely have been fortunate in having outstanding individuals serving on our staff throughout the years. With the changes in camp programs, the number of new faces on staff, each year, has increased. Since 2000, we have added staff positions to the following area:

Quartermaster; Trading Post; additional Life-Guards at aquatics; Shooting Sports; C.O.P.E and Climbing; SCSC area; M.A.D.E. area; the addition of a second Health Officer; Ranger Service and Food Service.

With the changes that have taken place over the years, the camp averages around 60 staffers each summer. As new merit badges are release and as new programs develop, that number will increase, as will the number of campers that come to the best camp in the Nation, Camp Rotary, the camp that we all love so well.

Andrew leading a campfire

CHAPTER 4

MY JOURNEY WITH THE LEGENDS THE MARV AND JUSTINE VALENTINE STORY

By Rich "Waz" Wasmer

INTRODUCTION
A PROUD SON REFLECTS ON HIS MOM AND DAD

Dad and Mom were both Marines, and very proud of it. They met in the Marine Corp in California after Dad returned from a tour in Korea. Mom got transferred to Pearl Harbor and I don't know how Dad did it but he "finagled" some orders and chased after her. They later married at the submarine base chapel in Pearl Harbor, and when they were discharged, they returned to Michigan where Mom was from. Dad started working for my Grandfather who was president and general manager of Koestlin Tool and Die Company in Detroit. Dad got his journeyman card as a skilled tradesman. When Dad was not working, we found ourselves on Lake St. Clair in my grandfather's boat. My first swimming lesson was being tossed from the boat into the lake, and Dad saying "sink or swim son, your choice." Of course he jumped in with me and I kind of swam.

As I got older, and into baseball, Dad also got into baseball, and started an American Legion baseball team in Mt. Clemens. Of course he had to have all the best equipment, and gave 100% to the boys. It is not surprising that his teams would always be front runners. I remember he had a pitching machine, and after his team was done with practice, it was my turn. Now I was in little league, and American Legion Baseball was high school. Well he cranked up the machine a little and told me to stand in the box, and just watch the ball. Whack! The first pitch hit me in the arm, and dad said you are a little close. After some coaching, I finally hit the ball. He said, if you can follow the ball at that speed, and hit the ball you will be good. Ooh…the memories.

Then I got into Cub Scouts with my Mom as my Den Leader, and that was the start of the Valentine scouting adventure. Dad started working with the Cub Scouts, and as I got ready for the Boy Scouts, Dad was not happy with the troop I was to join. He thought he could do better, so he started Troop 157 in the Clinton Valley Council. He started with just a few of us, and the troop soon grew to about 100 scouts. We were always doing something. We camped once a month regardless of what the weather was like. We did hikes and canoeing. And through it all he expected your best. If it was not your best, it was not good enough.

For summer camps we were part of a group that helped launch Lost Lake Scout Reservation. A couple of times Dad thought that he and the other leaders of the troop could take the troop on a great adventure, and we set off on our own summer camp at French Lake near Mackinaw. I am not sure how he found the place, but we were the only ones there for a week. We had canoeing, swimming, hiking and boxing. That week challenged us. He taught us not only camping, but ethics. Some of the lessons I did not understand at the time. Isn't it funny, how and when we get older, those silly lessons are something of great value as we do get older? Again his philosophy was "if it's not your best, it's not good enough."

In 1968, we loaded up his pick-up, and Mom, Dad, and I headed west to Philmont Scout Reservation in Cimarron, New Mexico. Mom and Dad attended training and I did the hike. What an adventure, and a blast! We camped along the way, and boy, we had fun. I remember on the way home, he saw signs about a big rodeo in Cheyenne, Wyoming. Although it was out of the way, he thought it would be a good family adventure, so off we went. When we got there, we found that the "big rodeo" was the week before, and all we seen were kids my age roping sheep. But it was an adventure! That was the first, and only "family" vacation that I remember. All of his other vacations were spent with the baseball team, and later with the boy scouts. Mom was always the supportive and faithful wife, and a loving and doting mother, and at times, a buffer between dad and me.

The year was 1969, and I was having fun in the neighborhood, but things were changing. After the Detroit riots, 2 years previous, things started to change. Crime was invading the area. Dad wanted to get us out of the big city. He wanted the best for us, and a good environment for me. He was now working for Chrysler as a "plank owner" of the Sterling Stamping Plant. He wanted better for his family.

Also in 1969 he formed a special troop of boys from the Clinton Valley Council to take to the 1969 National Jamboree in Idaho. What a trip, first class! We traveled by train from Chicago to Idaho with various stops along the way, including Glacier National Park. The gateway to our troop camp was a giant Boy Scout handbook that Mom and Dad spent weeks building and painting. You would enter and leave camp by walking thru the pages of the handbook. Another great adventure.

Then, along came Camp Rotary, an event that would change our lives forever. I remember hearing some talk between Mom and Dad about a possible move. I remember being very upset. I did not want to leave my

Grandparents, and going to high school with all my friends are all that I knew. I remember driving to that camp for a tour. NO HOUSE! Where were we to live! No neighbors, no friends! I did not want to move! WHY?!

Well Dad was hired, and he moved to camp staying in the health lodge. It was the middle of the school year, and Mom and I stayed in Mt. Clemens, while I finished school, and driving to Rotary on weekends. Dad's favorite meal was fried baloney on a 2 burner electric cook top. The adventure began. I had never seen so much snow. I remember the camp had a 2 wheel drive GMC pick-up that we used to plow with. And work! I learned how to work, and work hard. Again Dad would say if it's not our best, it's not good enough!

Camp is where I met my first honest to goodness Paul Bunyan lumber jack. A guy bigger than life! Mr. Terry Shull. Well as the story goes, Dad and Terry had a few "meetings" about camp hunting, and fishing, and soon became good friends. Terry had property that was adjacent to Rotary. Later Terry, and Dad dug the basement for a house.

The summer of 1970, mom, and I moved to camp. The first neighbor I met was Joel Magnus, the nephew of the camp cook Marion Magnus. Joel was a year older, and in Drivers Ed, and we became fast friends. One summer day, I was told that my friend Joel had died in a swimming accident. That was my first experience with death. Later that summer, Dad sent me off on an adventure by myself. I went to Schiff Scout Reservation in New Jersey for C.I.T. training. Upon my return it was time to go to work.

Dad introduced me to P. Karl Rowley, the Water Front Director at camp. That began another great camp adventure, and my love for the waterfront. Little did they know, a few years later, I would be part of the waterfront staff to start a revolution in renaming the swimming area the Water-back. Dad was not very happy to have the "order of things upset." But he eventually saw the light.

In the fall of 1970, I started school, and upon returning home from school, my real education would begin. Life at camp was always busy. Something was always going on, and things ALWAYS needed to be fixed, painted, made, and improved, and roads to be plowed, and graded. As I look back, Dad was always teaching little life lessons, although I did not see it at the time. I do not recall the year, but Dad said we needed to build

3 cabins. The foundations were poured for Chipmunk, Loon and Pike. The cabin was a pre-fab type, and the walls came in 8 foot sections. I learned a little about building from that experience. Then the snow started, and by the time we started working on Pike, the snow was so deep we had to haul wall sections in on snowmobile. It seemed like, during that particular winter, every day after school was spent working with Dad and others on the cabins. Again, little life lessons along the way.

We always had people at our home. Although I was an only child, our home always had "family" present.

Steve Gray is one such person. Steve lived at camp for some time and we became "brothers" quickly doing many things together, and setting out on our own adventures. Steve was a ranger, and helped Dad a lot. Steve is now the Maintenance Director for Newaygo County, Michigan.

Then there is Gabriel "Smew" Ismaio. Smew is from Libya, and was going to school at Central Michigan University when Col. Kaddafi came to power. Smew came to live with us at camp, and worked as the Kitchen Steward. We also became brothers. Gabriel now works for GM in St. Louis, Missouri, and Dad has flown out to see him and his family where Dad was treated like a king.

Throughout the years, when Dad became Camp Director, each and every staff member, became "family." Dad always demanded the very best of us. If it was not your best, it was not good enough. He expected 100% from all of us. We were, after all, there for the boy scouts, and they deserved the very best from each of us.

As I got older, and began to "find myself," we butted heads a few times, but Dad was always teaching life lessons. And although I did not realize it at the time, I mean, hey, I was a typical teenager and Dad did not know much. Isn't it funny how that works?

As I got older and the Vietnam War was going strong, I recall one night sitting around the TV watching the war draft. At the time each male at a certain age had to register for the military draft, and once each year they would televise the draft lottery. They would draw a name 365 times for each day of the year. The order in which your birthday was the order you would be drafted for the service. I know Mom was very nervous as was I. I had made the decision that I would never be drafted, and if the time came, I was going to enlist, and make Dad proud. Of course being a Marine was high on the list. My draft number was 156. Ironic that my troop number in Mt. Clemens was 157. I met resistance for enlisting, and from all people it was Dad. He had seen firsthand the horrors of combat, and I think it was his way of protecting me. I remember, he told me "not this war." I later understood his thinking. I remember one very specific conversation that I had with Dad. He never said anything about his combat experience. But Dad said, and I paraphrase, at times things are worth fighting for, God, country, family, and honor. You have to make the decision about your life. I have tried to give you guidance, but the choice is yours. Our country is not in it to win this one for whatever reason and too many good young men are dying. Not this war. Although Dad was not in favor of me enlisting, he did instill in me a sense of service; of giving back, and trying to make a difference. I think in a large part that is why I chose the fields I did, first as a Paramedic and then as a Public Safety Officer.

After I graduated and moved away to start my own life I always came "home to camp." Mom and Dad always gave their best to camp and to the scouting movement. Staff was always family, and home to many. There have been other sons, and a few daughters along the way, Erv Hutter, Tom Olver, Trevor Adcock, and Fred Engdahl, to name a few. I apologize for not naming all of them, but the list would be very long. And then there is Waz. Waz became a trusted family friend and Dad's sounding board, confidant.

There have been a few times over the years when I thought I was going to lose my Dad; his fall from the ladder, while cleaning the gutters at home, and suffering his head injury, and his subsequent heart surgeries. I'd like to thank one wonderful individual; thank you, Mr. Dick O'Dell for being there for Mom, and me during this trying time.

I have tried to live my life in a way that would make Mom and Dad proud. I have made mistakes along the way, but Mom and Dad have always been there if I needed them. They never tried to interfere in my life, relying on their love, guidance, Marine upbringing, and having the Scout Oath and Scout Law as my guide.

Since Dads retirement, Mom and Dad have had a good life, moving to their favorite area in Traverse City, and enjoying going out to dinner, and I think trying all the restaurants in the area. They made new friends at their summer place on Lake Leelanau. However some unexpected challenges have come their way. Mom was going through the beginning stages of dementia. I talked Mom and Dad into moving close to me so I could keep an eye on them. My Mother, who has been a Mother to so many over the years, who always had a smile, and opened her arms to so many in need, showed signs of getting worse. Dad did his best to care for her during the time, but it was wearing on him. Then in the fall of 2011 mom fell at home, and broke her hip, and underwent surgery. The illness got worse, and Dad and I decided that it would be best for Mom and him, that she be admitted into the long term care facility at the hospital in town. My wife Tracy and daughter Shawnna are hospital employees, and keep a constant eye on Mom. I am up there often, and Dad gets there a few times a week if not more. Mom has a hard time communicating. I do not think she really recognizes me or Dad or Tracy or the grandkids. But whenever she sees Dad, Tracy or me she seems to light up if only for a brief minute. She still has her smile, is hardly ever down, and is well cared for, and loved by all the staff. Having the love of his life "gone" has had a definite effect on Dad, but he carries on.

Camp, and all of the staff members, over the years, have meant so much to Mom and Dad. They have lived a life of unselfish service to others. They loved, raised, taught, and scolded many of us over the years. But we all learned little, and big life lessons along the way. Dad in his own way is still teaching me life lessons, and living with grace, and dignity. He is my best friend.

For the Valentine family, Camp Rotary will forever be our home. The memories and experiences that I had at camp, and lessons learned from my parents, and the Scout Oath and Law, will forever be the principals that will guide me for the rest of my life:

"If it's not your best, it's not good enough."

Gary Valentine, January 2013

AND SO THE JOURNEY BEGINS……..

"They put their heart and souls into a camp that they loved so well."

Marv and Justine Valentine were both serving with the United States Marine Corps when they married on Nov. 7, 1953. The following year, they both were honorably discharged, and returned to Marv's home state of Louisiana. Later on, an opportunity came for Marv and Justine to move to Michigan where he was employed as a tool and die maker. On November 22, 1955, their son Gary, a future Eagle Scout was born. Marv and Justine became very active volunteers in their community. He coached an American Legion Boys baseball team that went on to become state champions. They started Troop 157 in Macomb County with just 5 scouts, and grew to over 100 members. In 1969, Marv and Justine grabbed on to another opportunity and moved to Clare, Michigan. Marv had been offered a Camp Ranger job which eventually turned into the Camp Director position at Camp Rotary; a move that would not only impact their lives but many others as well. It was the beginning of an era of dynamic growth for Camp Rotary; an era when many camp traditions began. In 1970, the Valentine's on site living quarters were in the Carney Health Lodge. It was rough going for a while; the quarters were very small and not well insulated especially during the winter months when the water pipes kept freezing. He gained Council's permission to build a new home on the camp property just inside of the main gate. He and his neighbor, Terry Shull, dug out a basement for the new home forming its foundation. He also had the responsibility of building a new dining hall on the hill opposite from the old dining hall.

In 1971 Justine took over as Health Director during the summer months. She and Marv toiled endlessly in camp. Their vision was for camp to be the best scout camp in the nation. Marv oversaw the building of three new cabins on the property along with some pavilions and other structures. Their days were long; their sacrifices many. Marv, along with his close friend, Roy Chase, organized the Society of George. This was the second society that he helped form, the first being in Macomb. The Society of George recognizes active adult Scouters for their involvement and hard work on camp properties in keeping with the adage that "George will do it." The society is still very active today. He started Cub Day Camp and Webelos Camp. He served on Wood Badge Staff and the National Camp School Staff. He also initiated Rotary's Outdoor Education Program; served as Tomahawk District Executive for a time and along with his son, Gary formed Boy Scout Troop 620 in Clare, Michigan. These were just some of his many accomplishments during his 30 year span at camp.

MY START WITH THE DIRECTOR

I first met Marv in the spring of 1972 on Rotary's parade field. Marv was showing Art Henry around camp. Art had served as the Council Executive of the Paul Bunyan Scout Council and was well known for his collection of scouting artifacts, and his "Tin-Tent" that he and his family camped in. Art along with Jack Beamish, a legend at Paul Bunyan Scout Reservation, and I were at the dedication of the Paul Bunyan Scout Reservation during the summer of 1963. I was serving with the U.S. Air force at the time and was an Assistant Scoutmaster with Troop 101 from Wurtsmith Air Force Base in Oscoda.

Getting back to that particular Saturday afternoon in 1972, Marv asked me to serve on camp staff. I couldn't. I just didn't have the time. I was a Webelos Leader with Pack 3146, organized in part by Bette Hutter, in Bay City. I was also in the beginning stages of forming a new scout troop, Troop 103 and employed at a full time job in Midland. So, I decided to meet Marv half way by spending a week in camp with my new troop and volunteering my time with an additional week here and there each summer as a commissioner on staff. All Commissioners were volunteer staff during the Valentine years. I did this throughout the 1970's, 80's and 90's. During these years I met and worked with many dedicated scouters who all shared a deep love for the camp. These were devoted folks who all gave of themselves unselfishly to the betterment of Rotary. Some of the Scouters I remember serving on the Commissioner's Staff with:

Harold Schmidt	Gale Peters	Jake Hutter
Larry Jeziorski	William "Doc" Ferrell	John Raducha
Eldor Hutter	Ed McClure	Clarence Miller
Dick O'Dell	Don Lyons	Vern Yant
Ron Nowacyk	Glen Coveleski	And others…..
Jerry Eichinger	Jack Cambridge	

Over the years there have been other good hearted scouters who volunteered for every kind of camp project imaginable, not only at Rotary but also at Paul Bunyan Scout Reservation and Bear Lake Scout Camp. I apologize for not listing these dedicated folks, for it would require another book to do so, and also I have a fear of leaving someone out. Many are no longer with us. They were and are the true champions of scouting having served as Camp Masters and members of the Society of George and our OA lodges, and from the many faithful scout troops that kept returning to Rotary throughout the years.

One of the most demanding areas of camp to staff, which we all helped with, is in the camp kitchen. Work days are very long and tiring, and strong work ethics is a must. Good food quality and quantity had to be there, no exception; if not, other programs in camp could suffer if we had a poor evaluation in food service. Some of the dedicated cooks were: Charlot Wilcox; Marion Magnus; Gerry "Cookie" Hentschel; JoAnn Agin; Jackie Bourdon; Mary Schell; Dale Hays; Mary Kaufmann; Pat Currier; Cindy Izydorek; Betty Blake; Susan Anderson and Frank Cody.

In August of 2011, the cooks and kitchen staff really had to prove themselves. Rotary hosted an event that was unparalleled in its history with an encampment of the Church of Latter Day Saints scout troops from through-out Michigan, and neighboring states. Two gigantic tents with tables, and seating were set up on the parade field as their dining area. Sunday dinner, and Monday breakfast, the cooks, and staff served over 900 people, cafeteria style with six lines of campers going through three long buffet tables, in the dining hall, in less than 40 minutes. Later on Monday, and early Tuesday, a couple hundred or so of the campers went to PBSR for the rest of the week to engage in high adventure activities. That left around 700 campers to serve, at each meal, and the kitchen staff accomplished the feat in around 25 minutes. Throughout the week, Gordon's Food Service parked a trailer, filled with food, alongside the dining hall. It was a week that the cooks and kitchen staff proved their skills along with the rest of the camp staff and volunteers in the different program areas. Also hats off to Camp Director, Brad Murray and Program Director, Andrew Wright for leading a very successful week.

ON STAFF WITH MARV

It wasn't until years later in 1996 and after serving as a volunteer Summer Camp Commissioner for 24 summers that I was able to take Marv up on his offer, and became a full time staffer. I had retired from Dow Chemical the year before, and was ready or at least I thought I was. Under Marv's leadership being a Rotary Staffer brought on many challenges. Foremost, it was striving for perfection in putting on the best program possible. No doubt about it, solid programming was to be a tradition at camp no matter what area you worked in, as he believed, the camping experience should be of such a positive experience where each scout would have memories lasting a lifetime. To us staffers, that meant we were expected to give 100 plus percent, and do so, always with a smile, on any given day of a summer camp week. Going above and beyond was the norm, and he rallied us to insure that every camper had an experience that was top notched. Our days of summer were long ones as we were expected to perform to his level, because this Marine, who served so honorably with his Marine wife during the Korean conflict, would accept nothing less. His goals were high ones. Although we were always tired; he was too. But he never failed in taking the lead making it all come together. We were regulated by National Scouting Standards (standard operating procedures on the operation of a Boy Scout summer camp), which during camp staff week; he had us read, every dang word of it. Camp staff week (training for staff members) days were filled with class room instructions; much manual labor; setting up our skill areas, and getting the whole camp, and its programs ready for the campers. We were fortunate, at the end of any given day, to get to our bunks before midnight. I remember during one of those training weeks, we spent many hours, each day, digging trenches between each new staff cabin in staff village for the laying of electrical ground wiring. Talk about bull work. Mike Bingham and others would lay the electrical cord as the rest of us DUG! I also had the privilege of working with "master builder" Frank Gerace repairing the walk-over bridge going to Fort Scott. Frank was so much of a perfectionist that if I bent a nail, even slightly, he made me remove it and apply another. I learned much from this scouter extraordinaire. Also, during a big part of staff week, we ran the camp program for Rotary youth. This gave the staff in different skill areas the opportunity to run their programs before camp opened for the scouts.

Marv also led by his own personal code of conduct that he expected each of us to live up to. I should mention that if we performed to the best of our ability and it showed, he'd back us up. An example would be if a concern or complaint came down the pike questioning our performance, he would go to bat for us. So there was a perk in doing our jobs well. Believe me, it was always a good thing having Marv on our side than not. You always knew where he stood. He kept reminding us that the ONLY RULES of camp were the Scout Oath and the Scout Law. If we broke them, we knew where the camp entrance was. It was also the exit. And honestly, there were times when I would look over towards that camp gate asking myself, "What the heck am I doing here?" But I was able to put the little stress that we all shared, aside. But there were others who could or would not, and for them, old US-27, outside the gate was theirs to take.

Working at Rotary was an experience that impacted all of us in lessons of life. It was an era that many of us will value for a life time. Marv would permit us to make mistakes, but we had better learned from them, and they better not be repeated. And would you believe there was a lighter side to the man also? I'll cover that later. But what you saw is what you got; character, forthright, true to his word, solid example and hard, hard work. Camp Rotary was in his blood, and we never wanted to see that blood boil. His family was number one, and camp was a very close second (I think that's the order). His vision was for his beloved scout camp to be number "UNO," and to grow serving generations to come. And he expected everyone to set the presence in making that happen, or else!

A WALK IN HIS SHOES

Filling in for a Camp Director can be an experience beyond words. The position comes with tremendous responsibilities that can be downright stressful, as I found out. Before summer camp, I attended National Camp School for certification, but, it never prepared me for what was to happen. It was in 1998 and I was the Program Director, and just before the 4th week of summer camp, Marv got the "Bug." He was hit with some kind of virus, worse than the flu. He was definitely a sick puppy running a high fever, couldn't eat, and could hardly utter a word. The doctor confined him to his home prescribing antibiotics, and other meds. I did not see Marv face to face that entire week. We just conversed over the phone as I took on his directorship responsibilities. Dan Tanciar, from the office staff, was my assistant. We did everything, from running the daily round tables to ordering and picking up food for the dining hall to reacting to a lost bather at the Water-back, and trying our best keeping the staff focused. On top of it all, I would counsel the golf merit badge to 40 scouts each day. Much of Dan's and my time were spent with troop leadership putting out "fires" when there was a conflict between them, and the different skill areas, because of merit badge interpretation, or a "personality" problem with someone. We helped the health lodge with a few injuries that week. We had some severe storms come our way, and were in constant communications with the Sheriff's Department. We had an abusive situation in one campsite that we had to give priority to, having several meetings on. We had to reconcile the daily transactions in the Trading Post, and I ran the opening, and closing campfires. It was a very tiring and emotionally exhausting week for Dan and me. We were in direct contact, each day, with the Council Scout Executive with a "daily report." And of course, we kept Marv informed also. Dan and I relied on the professional support of the administrative team at the scout office; Linda, Norma, Jean, Misty and Birdie. These ladies always came through for us. Marv did get better, and was back on the job for week 5. Dan and I were grateful beyond words to be back "in our own shoes" again.

HE WANTED TO DO GOLF

It was either in the mid or late 1980's that I suggested to Marv that the camp get involve with the golf merit badge. I drew up a lesson plan from the Golf Merit Badge book. It was to be a 5 day merit badge. The class would practice in camp with their golf swings, and work on the requirements from the merit badge book. We drove balls at the football field under the guidance of a former staffer, Greg Heckathorn. Greg was a golf-pro in the area. One day a week we would go out to the driving range in Harrison. Another day we would go to Tamarack's Golf Course, and play a-round of golf. Now, Marv loved golf. Would you believe, along with his many responsibilities, he took over as the merit badge instructor? He continued teaching golf each summer until 1996 when I was hired on staff. I told him that I would be on staff on one condition. I wanted to do the golf. He reluctantly gave up the reins, and for the next seven summers I was the counselor for golf. Because of good marketing, and recruiting lots of adults from the different troops to assist, the golf program at Camp Rotary was extremely successful. Especially in 1997 in April, Tiger Woods, the youngest golfer ever to win the Master's Golf Tournament, had golfers, and non-golfers alike, throughout the Nation, in complete awe. Each Sunday, the scouts were arriving in Rotary's parking lot with their back packs, and golf bags filled with clubs. Golf during the summer of 1997 was the second most sought after merit badge right behind Wilderness Survival. Some adult golfing volunteers who assisted for years were Morgan McMann from Milan, MI., David Laabs, from Northville, MI. and Scotty McKinnon, from Bay City, MI. During the summer of 1997, I believe the 5th or 6th week of camp, there was a gentleman helping me with the merit badge. His son was in the class. His name was John Smith, and he had just transferred from General Motors Europe to GM Detroit, MI. He was a common Joe of a guy who could really relate to the scouts. He showed up every day, and we would divide our large class size into two with John taking one half, and me the other. We had great conversations during the week. We hit it off very well. It was a day, after summer camp, in September, back home, and the mail man knocked at my door in Bay City. He had an insured package that I had to sign for. It was from the General Motors Corporation, Detroit, MI. I opened the package and found a "Masters Golf Towel" along with a dozen "Masters" signature Golf Balls and "Masters" signature Tees. There was a typed letter directed to me thanking me for my time at Camp Rotary introducing and teaching the game of golf to so many young people. The letter was signed, John Smith, Office of the CEO, General Motors Corp.

WOOD BADGE AT ROTARY

"WHO HATH SMELT WOOD-SMOKE AT TWILIGHT?" WHO HATH HEARD THE BIRCH-LOG BURNING?" Back in August of 1974, I took Wood Badge Course, EC 40-19, at Rotary, back when the course was still a week long. Although Marv was not in charge of the course, he had a very high regard for Wood Badge, having served on previous wood badge staff. Charles Schroeder was the Course Director and Vince Waier was the Senior Patrol Leader. I was in the Fox Patrol. I remember the last day of the course, and we had to prepare a big meal for dinner. I was elected to do the salad as I had a reputation for making the best. Marv and Justine were our guests of honor for dinner. They commented that it was the best salad they had ever eaten. Wood Badge was a dynamic experience, especially at Rotary, and it motivated me beyond anything I've ever experienced in scouting. In the years following, for some reason, Wood Badge was no longer staged at Rotary. Many years it was held at Paul Bunyan Scout Reservation. Then in August of 1990 it returned to Rotary and I was appointed Wood Badge Assistant Course Director and counselor to the Beaver Patrol. What a privilege! Fred Berkman was the Course Director. It was more work preparing, and working wood badge staff than any other scouting activity that I've been involved in. It was a dynamic experience and well worth the effort.

THE WHEEL-BARROW SALAD

Back during the time, in the 80's and 90's, we had Junior Leaders Training for scouts. Some of the week-end training was held at Rotary but the week long training was at Paul Bunyan Scout Reservation. At one event, "Uncle" Howard Weidman, also known as "Mr. Dutch Oven," asked me to do the salad. It was when lettuce was over $2.00 a head. I went to Glen's Market in Mio, bought all the ingredients (cheeses, Italian meats, oil, vinegar and other vegetables) including two crates of lettuces. The bill was around $240.00 (cost more than the entrée of baked chicken and the fixings). I thought Uncle Howard was going to have a coronary. There were six of us volunteers cutting up the lettuce, meats and other vegetables working hour's non-stop. We had, LOTS, really lots of salad. Now what would I serve it in? I found an old used wheel-barrow on the property that I cleaned, and lined with aluminum foil. In the wheel barrow, I mixed the salad, and served it going from table to table among the hungry eaters. Everyone loved it. John Foltz, then OA Lodge Advisor, saw to it that the Wheel-Barrow Salad became a staple at OA Fellowships at the different camps. Marv loved the Wheel-Barrow Salad concept.

MARV TOOK PRIDE

Marv took pride with many of his staff people and often "adopted" some inviting them to live and work year-round on the camp property. Some of the staff to live year-round in camp was Tom Oleniacz, Erv Hutter, "Smew" Ismaio, Dale Klimmek, Fred Engdahl, Mike Murphy, Denny Tomkins, Steve Kastner, Frank Smekar, Gerald Cain and Dave Davis.

Marv took exception that if at any time, anyone found a single piece of paper on its 1100 plus acres; he took exception because we were trained along with the troops that if any foreign material were found on camp grounds, they would IMMEDIATELY BE PICKED UP AND PUT IN THE TRASH. Tents were to be straight, tied and aligned as best as could be. Because of the always tight camp budget, new tents were hardly acquired. Now enters, a legend in his own right, the "Bear." Over the years, Camp Ranger Art "Bear" Beck kept the old tents in fair condition as best as he could. In fact he kept the whole camp fixed as best as he could. Off, and on he would fill in as Shooting Sports Director. When that happened, Ranger Service was accomplished by either, Jerry Clarke, Mike Bingham, Gary Avery and Sons (The "Week-end Rangers) Stew Patterson or others. "Bear" took pride in "HIS" parade field, always planting new seed, and watering. He guarded and watched those working lawn sprinklers on the parade field like a hawk. Anyone caught playing with them received a loud, a very loud "verbal lashing." He would also pay close attention to the football field, mowing and watering, and retrieving golf balls from the merit badge class. Bear had a reputation of speeding in the camp's pick-up on the camp's roads. We always reminded scouts and scout Leaders, when they heard a vehicle approaching, while walking the roads, to step aside, and off the road, stop and face the moving vehicle. This rule worked out very well, especially when "Bear" was driving, not only did the scouts stop and look, they ran as fast as they could into the woods. ALL SKILL AREAS AND EVERY AREA OF CAMP WERE TO BE PREMIER AREAS OF SHOW, AND NEEDED TO BE NEAT AND CLEANED. Central Lodge's and its kitchen had to be swept, and cleaned on a continuous basis, and Marv would often supervise the mopping of the floors, like a manager hovering over his employees at a McDonald's restaurant. The physical facilities of each program area, each day, were to be in place, and the program started ON TIME! Staff had to go over their area lesson plans making sure no flaws came about. This was true for all programs in camp. Case in point, every Friday evening at campfire, we would have the Order of the Arrow "Tap Out" ceremony with three canoes of Native Americans, spaced apart from each other on the lake, paddling to the campfire bowl and arriving at the EXACT SAME TIME. With this particular Friday night ceremony, only two canoes did. One canoe had an inexperienced Jive paddling it going circular 360 degrees most of the time. It arrived a few minutes late. To add fuel to the fire (no pun intended), the kerosene that was used to soak the wicks on the torches that the Natives in the canoes would light, and carry, were damped with moisture. Only one torch would light. At the campfire bowl I looked over at Marv with his campaign hat on, studying the ground beneath his feet. I thought back to staff week, and staff training when a day would not go by without him reminding us to be PREPARED making sure nothing ever went wrong with any SEGMENT of the camp's program. Well, when we finally got through the OA ceremony, Marv dismissed the troops back to their campsites, and had the entire staff stay for a "productive" meeting that lasted well into the morning hours. To him, Camp Rotary was to be top performing, and anything less was unacceptable: unacceptable, indeed. During his tenure, he put his heart, and soul into the camp's program; every blessed single, detailed aspect of it.

HIS OTHER SIDE

No question about it. Marv's directorship was a firm one; the camp had a kind of regimentation to it (his military background, I supposed), and although he was never light on discipline; he showed another side, and a very welcomed one at that. "You should pay me for being here," a smiling Marv would tell his staff members. "Your work at camp is repetitious; your days long and there'll be good ones and not so good ones," he would say, "So, you need to make your job fun. And if you're not having fun, you need not be here." So, he would often take the lead during the camp week showing us how to have fun. At meal times, in the dining hall, we sang, and did stunts like "Where O' where is Susie?" And then, we would award the "Golden Banana." The Golden Banana was a form of recognition given to the quietest and cleanest table. Often Marv was the recipient to the fun stuff. He was a good sport when picked upon bringing laughs from the scouts and leaders. Every Friday, right after we ate, the staff would go all out putting on a "big show." A couple that I came up with was the $1.98 Beauty Contest, and the all-time favorite, the Gong Show. The Scouts ate it up. After the show, Marv would entertain the crowd with his favorite song, "Singing in the Rain." Then we all would stand, and with the staff leading from the stage, sing (with much enthusiasm) the "Y.M.C.A" song. And PIES! Marv and even Justine were hit with so many pies that it became a Friday dinner time tradition. Over the years they have had hundreds of pies thrown at their faces, and it always brought great response along with ROARS from everyone in the dining hall. At times, some of us brave enough would have concealed water pistols, and squirt anyone (not Marv) at random. We also threw water balloons on different occasions. Man, we certainly let our hair down. The energy was felt from the staff member to the scout to the leader. The noise coming from the Dining Hall, on Friday night, would echo throughout the whole camp. The fun times; there were many. And that is why, he would often comment, "You should pay me for being here."

PARADE FIELD FUN

At flag raising, and lowering each day, we would have staff messages. Staff messages were never to be referred to as "Announcements." If any person ever did, they would be subjected to the singing of "Here We Sit like Birds in the Wilderness," which is about four minutes of song that staff would sing out loud embarrassing the poor individual who verbally said "Announcements." Marv always wanted us to keep the messages short which we could never do. Back in the late 80's I started the "Good Scout" Award program. I handed out to the Scoutmasters, and Area Directors, Good Scout Awards to pass out during the camp week to a deserving scout on a daily basis. At evening colors, I would recognize the Good Scouts for the day. The recipients wore a little badge that they kept, and took home with him. It was a form of instant recognition that went over very well, well into the 2000's. To this day, folks come up to me saying how well they remember receiving the award, and how much it meant to them. On Saturday mornings, after the water carnival, the camp held the closing ceremony, and colors. Many area awards were presented along with the prestigious "Silver Axe Award." This was awarded to the best all-around troop in camp. Marv would only allow one award per camp week. Once (after a great deal of debating the point) he permitted two troops to receive it when the Camp Commissioners would absolutely not do a tie-breaker. The Silver Axe was replaced in 2000 when the new Camp Director, Ed Hoolehan asked me to come up with a weekly award that would recognize more troops for their involvement, and performance, not just awarding one troop during the week. The Award of Merit was established with Gold,

Silver and Bronze ribbons being awarded to scout troops. Just about all the troops earned a ribbon. The highlights on the parade field were stunts, and they were numerous. On Thursdays, we always held a scout leaders versus staff shoot out at the rifle, and archery ranges. Whoever lost the competition were the recipients of iced cold buckets of water. Now, the staff did lose a good percentage of the time. So picture the staff kneeling down in front of the whole camp with the winning scout leaders dumping one pail each over the fully uniformed staff members. What a sport Marv was; he always got soaked as well even if he didn't participate in the shootout. And water balloons! Especially on hot days. Over the years there were thousands tossed on the parade field. In promoting the Golf Merit Badge, throughout the week, I would have an "expert golfer" drive a golf ball into Lake Beebe. Much of the time, the golfer would hit one soaring beyond the floating docks. But on one occasion, staffer Tom Olver, who considered himself another "Tiger Woods," INSISTED on driving a ball. He took his stance, and with a perfect wide golf swing, connected off the tee with the ball going air-bound. It would have been a perfect drive for distance, except for one thing; the flag pole was in the way. With the ball traveling at great speed, and height, it hit mid-way to the top of the flag pole with much impact, ricocheting, just missing the heads of the three hundred plus scouts, and scouters standing in formation (OMG)! If the staff was going to pull a stunt on Marv and Justine, without them knowing, we'd have to keep it from them, and that wasn't easy. Marv and Justine, especially Marv had a gift to sense that "there's something brewing in these here woods." He completely despised not being in the know. This made it even more fun catching him and Justine off guard. At one evening flag ceremony, the staff spread the word to all the troops that everyone on the parade field would fall on cue when the firing of the cannon went off. The stunt went over without a flaw, the cannon sounded, and all 400 or so campers including the staff fell to the ground leaving Marv and Justine standing with dropped jaws. This brings to mind another similar incident, noticed I said incident, not stunt, to mind; an incident that I describe as being sad, because it makes one stop in his tracks to think about this changing world, and the direction that it is taking. It was mid-week during summer camp, week #8 (I believe in 1997) that an inter-city troop with 9 boys from Saginaw came to camp. They arrived on a Wednesday afternoon just before camp's evening colors, and chow. This was their first experience at summer camp, and maybe for many of them, their first time away from their home turf. On the parade field, we all lined up for formation. The regimentation confused them a little. So we helped, getting them lined up for the flag lowering, trying our best to make them feel at ease. With the camp facing the flag, the command was given "Scout Salute." The cannon sounded, and we all heard a loud "thump." Looking out of the corner of our eyes, while still saluting and the bugle blasting, as the flag descended down the pole, that loud "thump" noise was the 9 inter-city boys from Saginaw, together, all hitting the ground to the prone position. We should have warned them about the cannon. Their reaction to the cannon still sticks with me today,

During the mid-90's, another great stunt occurred one evening at Flags. Larry Jeziorski, a scout master and close friend, with his troop from Bloomfield Hills, brought a toy pink flamingo to camp and parked it outside of his tent in Schuck campsite. The bird would always come up missing, and throughout the week, on any given day, a ransom note would show up, and a staff member would read the note at dinner time. Larry and I had a heck of an idea. We contacted Scout Leader/police officer, Lt. Jeff Goyt (soon to be the Clare County Sheriff) to help us with our nasty little prank. At evening flag, the cannon sounded, the flag descended down the pole; and while staff messages were being read, from a distance came the sounds of two Clare County patrol cars with sirens on. Everyone was silent on the parade field as the two county patrol cars drove up, and onto the field. Everyone, except Larry and I of course, could not believe what they were seeing. The officers exited their vehicles, and walked up to Marv and Justine. Jeff read them their rights, and told them to turn around as he, and the other officers handcuffed them. Marv asked "What the Dang is going on?" Jeff replied, "You and Justine are being arrested on felony charges of kidnapping a pink flamingo." "A pink flamingo!" Marv shouted back, "I don't know NO DANG BIRD!" Handcuffed, Marv and Justine were escorted to the patrol cars and drove off. I dismissed the camp for din-din (dinner). A short time later, Jeff and the other officers brought Marv and Justine back to the dining hall. Marv took it all in good stride, just as a good sport would. Larry Jeziorski, and I would do other "fun" things throughout the camp week also. One I can remember was telling a camp fire tale of the "Camp Rotary Chain Saw Massacre" to a bunch of troops at Burrows Campsite. After the camp fire, I walked out of Burrows with a visiting troop over towards Schuck Campsite. Now, Larry had stationed himself in the woods a few hundred yards from Burrows, and with chain saw in hand, in the dead of night, started the loud thing. I just about got tramped. The screaming scouts made an immediate about-face, running as fast as they could back to Burrows.

THE STUNT OF ALL STUNTS

I didn't think anything would ever outdo the pink flamingo stunt. But I had another balmy of an idea. One week in July, during the summer of 1998, Rich Singer, a former SCSC staffer and a scout leader from Saginaw, and a Major in the Air National guard, divided his camp week up between camp, and his military training at Camp Grayling. It was on a National Camp Inspection day (boy that was brave of us) and the Inspectors departed right after lunch, therefore we were safe. However, we did include the Council Executive in on the surprise, and he stayed for the event. It was during evening flag that the ultimate of all stunts took place. A military helicopter was to make a low fly-over while the camp was assembled on the parade field. Major Singer was aboard the chopper, and on cue, I and some staff members moved the scouts and scout leaders back to a safe distance as the big bird landed, just to the west of the flag pole. Everyone stood in awe with mouths opened wide. Marv was dumbfounded. Out from the flying machine walked Major Singer, and other Air National Guard men. Marv invited the airmen to have dinner with us after which they introduced themselves, and spoke to the scouts about their military experiences. Upon dismissal from the dining hall, most of the camp ran to the landing pad where the Airmen permitted the Scouts to climb inside the helicopter for a real feeling of the big bird. Afterwards, the helicopter, with crew, ascended from the ground for its flight back to Camp Grayling, but not before performing some low fly-overs as the camp cheered and waved. It was a day that none of us will ever forget, especially the Valentines.

MORE MEMORIES

One week during summer camp in 1996, on a Thursday evening, I would be out at the P.A.T.H. overnighter telling my goose-bump stories. Don Thayer, our volunteer maintenance staffer had a farm in Clare where he raised LLamas. I asked him to bring a couple of them in to entertain the P.A.T.H. scouts. You should have seen the P.A.T.H. scouts out in North Camp when the Llamas arrived in their area. North Camp turned into a real petting zoo. I asked a lady scout leader from Lyle Tincknell's troop 186, Lake Orion, MI, to walk the llamas from the parking lot to North Camp. She agreed, and also led them around to some campsites. Can you imagine a young scout writing home to his parents saying "Camp was fun today, swimming, archery, and petting the llamas outside my tent?" It was a pretty unique attraction for a Boy Scout camp. Marv was out of camp at the time; I don't know if he ever found out about the llamas. But knowing the man, he probably did.

Under Marv's direction, the Friday night campfires were for the scouts and they had to be inspirational ones. He wanted to impact the audience to a high degree, after all; this was their last night in scout camp. From his traditional handkerchief cheer, "Remember, it's when the handkerchief leaves the hand" to the magical lightning of the friendship fires, and group songs to the staff skit (always with a message) to the OA ceremony, and then finishing up with the singing of scout vespers, he wanted the scouts and leaders to remember their week at Rotary. Thus an inspirational and fun last-night was his way of ensuring a wrap up to a great camping experience.

Over the years, I and others put together some great Friday night staff skits that always delivered a message; skits like "Touched by an Angel" and a "Tribute to Marv and Justine." Perhaps one of the greatest staff skits of all times was the "Wizard of Waz." This was a production that took much effort, much practice. It was the brain child of Staffer Tom Olver who got the idea from the Wizard of Oz. I don't know where Tom got the authentic costumes from, but they looked like the original ones from the Wizard of Oz movie set. Tom was the Lion; Jason Morrisette, the Scare Crow and Don Churchill, the Tin Man. I of course was the Wizard of Waz. It was a "Broadway Event," and a production beyond anything ever seen at a Friday night campfire. It took many hours of practice during staff training week and also into week one and two of summer camp. The word must have gotten out because every Friday night we had standing room crowds. To this day, folks still talk of the "Wizard of Waz."

EARLIER MEMORIES

Some of the earlier memories of the Valentines really do stand out. I remember Marv riding his favorite horse, Chip. Marv had a small fenced-in area for Chip by his house, and a much larger one out by North Camp. His pet dog, Smurf was a very smart dog, but always barking. But some of us staffers got to know Smurf's weakness. He enjoyed eating Wendy's hamburgers. If we knew we were going to be late getting back to camp, after having part of an evening off (a break outside of camp that all of us craved for), we'd bring Smurf a Wendy's burger, and he wouldn't bark, waking the Valentine's up. There was only one place to sign in, and out of camp, and that sign-out clip board hung by the front door to the Camp Director's house. Every once in a while that clip board would not be signed by staff personnel going in or out because (now, this is hard to believe) some staff personnel would skip out late at night when they were supposed to be in camp. Most of the time, Marv was apt to find out. Usually, nothing could escape the Camp Director. Any type of shenanigans that went on, he would in some manner, at least 90% of the time, find out sooner or later. And if it was sooner, as with staff leaving camp without permission, he would jump on his motorcycle traveling to Clare or Harrison; scouting the streets searching for his "lost" staff. Often he would locate them. Marv would first check Snow Snake Mountain Restaurant and then the White House Eatery. These two places were popular with the staff and opened 24-7. Needless to say, if any staff member were caught in this situation, it would not be a good thing.

In the 70's through 90's, at the end of summer camp, and after the last of the scouts returned home, it was a tradition that some of us adults visit a local establishment; after all, it was a long dry summer for us. Once or twice, if we were brave enough, we'd venture over to a club on M-61, a mere 17 minutes (got that down pat) from the camp gate. Although I was in civilian attire, and scout camp had ended, I still considered myself a representative of the BSA and would always act as so. But my fears were set aside, when, on our first visit, we bumped into some adult staff from PBSR.

One summer camp week in July, either the late 80's or early 90's, the camp staff was involved in a Halloween event hosting a costume party at the dining hall. For the party, Marv wore, well; it's really about what he didn't wear, and then who he ran into outside the dining hall. He went to the party portraying a baby, wearing only an adult diaper, and carrying a very large baby bottle with a big nipple. Long-time Nature Director Brad Coulson had invited a local Catholic Priest, and a Nun to visit camp. It wasn't good timing for them or Marv. As the Priest and Sister walked towards the dining hall, Marv was walking out, and as they met, Marv, with a big smile, introduced himself as the Camp Director. I don't know how well that went over, and I don't know who was more embarrassed, Marv or Father or Sister?

One afternoon during the last camp week in August of 1992, Mark Sprygada, a professional photographer, and scout leader from Bay City was walking around camp taking photos. From a distance, on the parade field, he saw Marv dressed in uniform with his campaign hat on sitting on the small stone wall in front of the Stewart's cabin. A young scout approached Mav, and as they were talking, Mark captured their picture. It was and is today, a classic photo that sends a message of the character of this legendary Camp Director.

In October of 2012, I asked Marv what he thought of his life so far. In his early 80's at the time, he pondered and replied, "Life's been good to Justine and me. I have no regrets. It's too bad that life has taken a turn in having Justine in a nursing home. Next November will be our 60th anniversary. I would give up my life, right now, if her situation could be different. It's very lonely for me without her. So, putting it aside, and having had her with me all these years, and being director at the best scout camp in the Nation, I'd have to say, it's been one good ride."

CAMP ROTARY'S MOM

The saying goes "Behind every successful man, there's a good woman." Over the years, Marv could not have achieved all that he had if it were not for the one who stood faithfully by his side, his love of life, and best friend, his spouse, Justine; together, since 1953. Together, as Marines serving their Country, and raising a devoted son, together as contributing citizens to their community, and serving scouting and their beloved Camp Rotary.

MARV, JUSTINE AND WAZ', August 2013

THEIR FINAL CAMPFIRE

It was quite an honor being Rotary's Program Director with the Valentines during their last year at Rotary. I wanted their last campfire in camp to be a very special one. So, let's go back to Friday, August 13, 1999 (yes I said Friday, the 13th) and their final campfire of their summer camp career highlighting their 30 years. This special fire marked more than 500 campfires that they had resided over. This was Marv's last time doing the magical lightning of the friendship fires; his last handkerchief cheer, and the last in taking the used ashes from the fires into his ladle to be used at future campfires. It also marked the last time he would be standing with his staff singing scout vespers while dismissing the troops back to their campsites. We had many folks standing in the antitheater that night; it was overflowing. Those who were lucky enough to get seated were packed-in like sardines. What a campfire this was to be. Just picture a beautiful clear, warm evening with the reflections of the trees on Lake Beebe. The moon, full as it could be as you watched the ambers of friendship fires die down. What an awesome sight indeed. BUT it wasn't like that at all! At dinner time, I kept glued to the weather report which was saying, "Expect storms in Clare and Harrison; some could be severe at times; high winds gusting in excess of 30 miles per hour and hale could develop. Take necessary precautions, and go to a low lying area if needed." The storm warning, would you believe, was for 9:15 P.M. lasting until 11:30 P.M. How ironic was that? Now I have to say that my stomach was in a knot. What would we do if a storm hit? There was no plan B. There was no room in the dining hall for everyone. This was Marv's last campfire, and we had to pull it off. We had numerous guests from all over the state of Michigan including Marv's personal friends, and a surprise visitor, his son, Gary. But the odds were quickly stacking against us. And on top of it all, it was, remember, Friday, the 13th. Evening came; the color of the sky was not good. It was 9:15 P.M., the troops with their ponchos, and the guests with their umbrellas, were walking to their seats in the amphitheater as the sky started darkening even more, and the winds picked up. We got through the opening, and the lighting of the fires, but now we heard thunder in the distance. Next the staff skit and then we saw the lightening not too far away. Next was the OA tap out ceremony, and the winds picked up even more as we heard rain coming down in force on the roof of the Central Dining Hall. Were we going to make it? We heard the rain hitting the roof of the Trading Post, and it was pounding down hard. But, we got through with the ceremony, and started Marv's, and Justine's tribute as the rain started pouring on the trees, and branches all around us. Would you believe, we finished the tribute, and aside from a few drops, no one really got wet! Rain was coming down hard into the lake, and it was thundering, and lightening as well, but not in the campfire bowl. As we sang scout vespers, and as Marv, for the last time, started dismissing the troops back to their campsites, I looked up, and thanked God for not allowing it to rain on the Valentine's parade. That was on Friday evening, August 13, 1999.

THE TRIBUTE

I called Marv and Justine up to the front to the campfire bowl. I began, "After all of you, scouts, and scout leaders are gone on Saturday; the camp with its skill areas, and camping sites emptied, and dining hall and parade field silent, it will be somewhat emotional for many of us. As we look throughout the camp, we'll still be able to hear the laughter, and joyful sounds, and see the smiles of the scouts whose lives we touched this past summer. Now multiply that by the many weeks in the past 30 summers that Marv and Justine have spent at camp, and imagine how they must be feeling right now. We believe that they will be linked with Camp Rotary as long as there is a Camp Rotary, and that they will be legends. Their unending dedication to Camp Rotary will be a big part of its history. Their drive for perfection in giving scouts the best summer camp experience possible will be their legacy." And I continued, "Anyone who has ever camped by our beautiful lake, and heard the loons; or watched the sun setting over the green hills, and tall pine trees, will remember you and your lady at your side. We bid you both farewells, our two dear friends. We thank you for the memories that you have given us. And to the tens of thousands of scouts you have served, may your rewards be tenfold. Camp Rotary will not be the same. But because of your hard work, your sacrifices, and your vision, Rotary will remain, and continue on to be one the of the greatest scout camps in the Nation for generations to come. God be with you both, in good health and prosperity. All of us will miss you both, immensely."

Out of the Valentine era came many camp traditions that are still with us today. They were wonderful years, and anyone who served on staff during those years will have memories lasting a life time. Since Camp Rotary first opened, it has been fortunate to have solid leadership coming from its many camp directors. But none of those directors lived the story as long as the Valentines. They sacrificed and toiled endlessly, impacting many lives. Their Legacy will be with us as long as there is a Camp Rotary.

"Softly falls the light of day,
While our campfire fades away."

"Remember, it's when the handkerchief LEEAAVEES the hand!"

CHAPTER 5

THE LEGEND OF LOST LAKE AND HARRY BENNETT

By Rich "Waz" Wasmer

Lost Lake Scout Reservation, part of the old Clinton Valley Boy Scout Council, and now part of the Great Lakes Field District, is located in Lake, Michigan, west of Farwell, Michigan. Lost Lake is a very unique Boy Scout Camp which opened in 1966. You're probably going to ask, why have I included a story of another scout camp in a book of Camp Rotary? Marv Valentine and his son Gary and their troop attended the camp when they were in the Clinton Valley Council and contributed much to its success in the early years. Also, Lost Lake and Camp Rotary had a relationship of sorts over the years. We were rivals and very competitive camps. Lost Lake covers over 2800 acres of beautiful forest land including three lakes. It is rustic camping at its best with spacious campsites; a tree tent village and the first camp in the Nation to offer "Tree Climbing." It also has something else that sets it apart from other scout camps; an unusual, and really awesome attraction. On the property over-looking the main lake, Lost Lake, is the former lodge and "fortress" of Henry Ford's right hand man, and director of Ford Motor Company security, Harry Bennett. The old lodge has a very intriguing past. I spent four years as the Program Director and/or the Assistant Camp Director, and instructed the Golf Merit Badge at Lost Lake.

In 2011, the lodge, because of its historical attraction, was featured in Scouting's National Magazine. The lodge has secret passage ways, and tours could be arranged in any given month. I personally gave tours of the lodge. The scouts were always fascinated in the structure as it was kind of spooky inside, especially in the basement. This gave me the opportunity to ad-lib somewhat, incorporating a ghost story that blended-in well along with the tour dialog. Believe me; I had the scout's attention especially with a wooden coffin, from a camp skit, that the Camp Ranger kept in the basement. The camp is a mere 30 minute drive from the gates of Rotary.

ROTARY vs LOST LAKE

Over the years, especially in the 70's through the early 90's, Camp Rotary's relationship with Lost Lake was extremely competitive and fun, and sometimes filled with mischiefs as both camps would occasionally pull pranks on each other. The staff from each camp would designate a prank night without the other camp knowing, and then enter either camp in the early morning hours to do its shenanigans. The staffers from both camps were really absorbed in this activity; I guess it was a way of them "letting go." Pranks consisted of sending camp equipment into the lake; untying canoes and row boats; using caution tape, and taping skill areas; raising foreign objects (like personal underwear) up flag poles; stacking tables, and other equipment into pyramids; toilet papering areas, and placing objects on roof tops. Staff members from each camp often knew each other, and were never destructive to either camp. Each summer it was common for us to get together at either camp for a softball game or tug-of-war, and other activities.

LOST LAKE AND HARRY BENNETT

While on staff, my living quarters were in Bennett Lodge. My wife would join me for a few days each week. Her first visit to the lodge was somewhat monumental. Right off the kitchen was a bathroom. She entered the bathroom one afternoon, and immediately exited asking, "Who placed that rubber snake on the floor?" I replied, "Rubber snake?" A friend and I both entered the bathroom together. Sure enough, on the floor laid a snake about 20 inches long. Only it wasn't 20 inches of rubber. It was real, and it was crawling. Just by the size of it, and its coloring, we knew it wasn't of a garden snake or milk snake variety. I asked my friend to pick it up. "I'd rather not, Waz," was his quick reply. We found an empty cardboard box, and somehow forced the reptile to crawl into it. We closed the lid to the box, and carried it outside; when from within the box, we heard the loudest rattling noise. We dropped the box, and ran with the snake escaping in one direction, and us in another. It was my first encounter with a Michigan rattler, commonly known as a Massasauga rattlesnake. Needless to say, my wife never did use that one bathroom again.

The following is taken from excerpts from the Detroit Free Press, dated Sunday, May 1, 1966, and from the Clare County Review dated Monday, May 9, 1988:

"Lost Lake Scout Reservation, with a concrete house and a 128-foot pouch was once the playground of controversial Detroit auto executive Harry Bennett. Bennett can be traced back to this area until around 1960.

Bennett, who was the right hand man of Henry Ford I, turned a one-bedroom cabin into a palatial estate fortress in the 1930's. Bennett bought the place from former Detroit Police Commissioner, John Gillespie. Although Bennett may have been a mystery man, his house stands as testimony to a bygone era from a time when auto executives could build monuments.

Older local residents can remember driving past the estate in the 1940's when the roads in this southern Clare County area were not much more than cow paths. When the residents saw the large wrought iron gate saying "Bennett" over the driveway, they were very impressed that this man had money. Long-time Clare County residents tell of armed guards patrolling the estate, of secret passageways, high-staked gambling and illegal moonshine whisky on the estate of Harry Bennett.

Bennett, who was an executive at Ford Motor Company during the 1930's and 1940's, was known for his union busting tactics which made him a foe of the United autoworkers. When Edsel Ford died in the early 40's Henry Ford was ready to make Bennett president of Ford Motor Company. However, through the urgings and finally threats of both Edsel's widow and Henry's wife, he decided against such a move.

Bennett had other large homes in the Detroit area which reportedly had secret passages that would allow Bennett to escape unnoticed from the home. One of those homes was located on the Detroit River and stories abounded in Detroit about the secret passage that led to a boat well. His other home was located along the Huron River in Ann Arbor.

Bennett was a figure surrounded by mystery. He has been the subject of many authors and his name is mentioned in most books concerning the Ford Motor Company and family. Harry Bennett also had a habit of socializing with known mobsters in Detroit including the Purple Gang, members of which frequented his concrete palace. Local legend had it those foes of organized crime in Detroit often ended up at the bottom of Lost Lake in "cement shoes." Since no remains have ever been found by divers, it remains another of the powerful myths that surround the Bennett mystique.

Following the death of Edsel in 1943, Henry Ford II, with the help of his mother and grandmother, wrestled control of the company away from his aged grandfather. As the company's new president, his first task was the acceptance of his grandfather's resignation from Ford and the second was the firing of Harry Bennett. Angry and humiliated, Bennett retreated to his Clare County home directing its completion. However, within days of his termination, work on the lake stopped because most of the workers were Ford employees diverted to finish Bennett's house with old Henry's approval. How or who finished the work on the home is unknown, but a few years later, Bennett walked out of the house fortress, never to return. He later retired to Desert Springs, Nevada where he died in 1985 of old age and penniless.

Lake, Michigan, Postmaster, Wilbur McLane, recalled how on a cold snowy night in the early 1940's, his father was summoned from bed to pull two Ford Motor Company semi-trucks several miles to US-10. The vehicles had become stuck in snowdrifts along North Lake Avenue while on a secret midnight delivery to Bennett's house. The drivers were invited to spend the night because of the terrible weather, but said that they couldn't because the two trucks had to be back in Dearborn before the morning shift, so they wouldn't be missed. McLane's father was offered a hundred dollar bill for each truck if his horses could get the vehicles to the payment which he did.

The main house is constructed of brick and block with concrete siding fashioned with details to make it look like split logs. An Italian immigrant employed by Ford Motor Company did most of the masonry work. Bennett discovered the Italian working at the Rouge Plant and sent him to work on the house. Local residents say the craftsman was so good, he quickly mixed bathes of cement and fashioned the concrete logs including the knots with a hand trowel. The roof of the home was replaced because its flat contours allowed ice and snow to collect and leak into the building. It took more than seven tons of shingles to cover the expanse of the roof. Local rumor had it that the roof was designed to ward off an invasion and at one time there were machine gun mounts on it. Others say the roof was used as a patio, complete with barbecue grill. An outside staircase constructed and fashioned to resemble to the rest of the house is the only route to the top.

The main lodge is built of reinforced concrete shaped like logs. It has eight rooms, five fireplaces and a main hall 60 feet long. Inside the house are six bathrooms and four bedrooms, three containing its own bathtub and fireplace. The two main fireplaces of the house are located in the dining room and living room. The master bedroom has a clear view of the largest of the three lakes, Lost Lake, which is 66 acres. The 128 foot screened porch overlooks the lake.

The floor of the living room is made of flagstone and is recessed near the fireplace, creating a sunken living area accommodating several semi-circular couches. In the main room there is a large table called a "whittler's bench." The top lifts up to reveal a large compartment, which allegedly held machines guns and other weapons. It was designed so well that to the average eye it appears to be an ordinary table for card playing or dining. A local craftsman, who was helping to install a refrigerator, tells of a guard lifting a tabletop and taking out rifles that were hidden there. Craftsmen, brought up from Greenfield Village, built most of the furniture. Only trees from the estate were used as lumber in the furniture.

At one time, Bennett thought of putting eight-foot chain link fence around the property. The cost was not even a consideration because a Ford warehouse in Dearborn was full of posts and fencing. However, conservation officials wouldn't allow the fence to go up because it would have seriously hampered the migration of deer.

The property had a swimming pool, which has deteriorated with time and was built on a whim. One day Henry Ford suggested that Bennett needed one so his guests wouldn't have to swim in what was a sometimes-dirty lake. Ford construction workers started on the pool later in the day. The pool was kept constantly filled by an artesian well which must have made for chilly dips when it wasn't heated.

A hidden passage led around and under the pool from the basement of the house to a dressing area and bar which used to boast a glass window where Bennett and the guests would sit and drink and watch the swimmers frolic. However, the window was removed during the renovation of the pool in the 1970's. The pool also had the capability of being heated in the winter but the cost was astronomical.

Bennett's original idea was to dredge the entire area around the house creating an island using the lakes tributary systems. A wide canal encircles half the house while the rest is slightly more than a choked swale. The dream, like other Bennett plans, was cut short by his firing from Ford.

Much of the equipment, money, materials and manpower put into the construction of the Bennett estate came from Ford Mother Company on the sly. Henry Ford I was aware of what was going on, but chose to look the other way. After all, Bennett was his fair-haired boy and head of Ford security. At any one time, Bennett bragged that he had access to almost a million dollars in his private safe for payoffs. Much of that money found its way into Bennett's personal collection of houses and cars which cost a fortune to maintain. In the end though, Bennett died penniless. When Bennett walked out of the house, he left behind food, clothes, expensive paintings, books and other household items. The estate was later sold to a Detroit steel company.

In 1965, Clinton Valley Council learned that the company was interested in selling the property. The council agreed to pay $350,000. In addition to the lodge, there are three lakes, a large bunkhouse, and a four-runway airport. The lodge overlooking Lost Lake is more than a mile from the nearest paved road. Scout officials stated that it would be at least mid-1967 before the property will be ready for organized camping and launched a $550,000 fund raiser to cover the initial cost of the development.

There is a good beach near the lodge and tents can be put up in the woods and clear areas. Scout troops will be able to use the property during the summer of 1968, although they will have to bring along their own gear."

Erv Hutter related that while Mrs. Ford played a part not allowing Harry Bennett to become president of Ford Motor Company there were other factors preventing him from being President also. W.W.II was under way, and war production was job one at Ford during the time. When Edsel Ford died, the Roosevelt Administration stepped in. They actually nationalized the company so that old Henry couldn't step back into any leadership role. Henry II was recalled from the U.S. Navy by FDR himself, and installed by the government as the acting president of Ford Motor Company on the condition that old Henry and Harry Bennett were to be removed from all official connection with the company. Henry II had no problem with any of this, he had a great disdain for his grandfather, whom he felt drove his father to an early grave, and he absolutely disliked Bennett. Bennett was fired, and manually expelled from the company offices.

THE VOLUNTEERS, LOST LAKE'S FINEST

Lost Lake had a big following of troops and individuals. All were hard-working and focused on improving a camp that they loved so well. During my tenure on staff there was William "Bill" Fortier who served as the Shooting Sports Director for more than 27 years. Bill a highly decorated soldier (numerous Purple Hearts and battle ribbons), fought for his Country in Europe during W.W.II. A very humble person, he would never talk about his war-time experiences. He made an impact on everyone he came in contact with. He was an inspiration; a hero, and a legend. Another was Fred Bond, who volunteered his maintenance services to the camp for more than 30 years. An electrician by trade, Fred could just about fix anything in camp, and would do so, many times, at his own expense. Another is Curtis Davenport; scouter extraordinaire, and a dynamic, enthusiastic individual. A former police officer, turned educator, who could rally the scouts like no other leader I have known. There was Bob Evans and his side kick, Jim Platt, two Canadian Scouters, who volunteered their time along with Kelly Martin, alias Santa Claus. And then there were the Jeff's, Gary's, Brad's, Art's, Bruce's, Michael's, Nick's, Ted's, Chris's, Jason's, Alex's, Johns, Rick's and many others. These were some of the folks who influenced me, but there were others whom I never met, all who played a big part, since 1966, in making this camp the outstanding, dynamic facility it was.

THE LODGE TODAY

Bennett Lodge intrigued me. I could not let go of the history surrounding it. Harry Bennett was born in 1892 and raised in both the Pinckney and Ann Arbor areas and died in 1985 without a dime. The roof top to Bennett Lodge is unsafe and a barricade was put in place years ago to prevent anyone climbing the cement steps to the flat roof. There is only one secret passage that's still operational located in the basement. It is actually a wooden bookcase that opens to a forward position leading to a winding stairwell to a lower level of the basement, and under the pool area. The swimming pool was used by the camp up to the early or mid-1970's, I'm told, and then filled in with sand and dirt. The cement steps on the stairwell were intentionally made for uneven stepping in case anyone would have made it that far in trying to apprehend Bennett. From the stairwell Bennett would run to his motor boat that was docked on Lost Lake. He would then take the boat to the other side of Lost Lake where his Ford was waiting for a fast escape to his airstrip and his plane.

The 128 foot screened in porch is still there but the section screens are torn apart or missing. Much cement around the building is cracked or chipped away. Some of the original wooden furniture, crafted from trees on the property is still in the home. The artesian well, outside of the home is inoperable or dried up. There were some old photos of Bennett and his family and other artifacts in the home. The whittler's bench, the table, with the top that lifts, where he supposedly stored his guns is in good condition and located in the main living room. This table, built by a company in Detroit, is quite a conversational piece.

NOW ONLY A MEMORY

From my personal perspective, the estate today is in terrible shape, and much capital would be needed for renovation. Because of its history, it would be a total injustice not to have pursued restoring this work-of-the-art structure which should have been accomplished years ago. Now, renovation, most likely, will never happen. Clinton Valley Scout Council ceased to exist after combining with the Detroit Area Council, and the two councils became the Great Lake Council, and then the Michigan Cross Roads Council. Under this new merger, Lost Lake Scout Reservation closed its gates in 2012. This beautiful and majestic property will only be a memory to the thousands fortunate enough to have experienced this jewel of a scout camp.

The closing of Lost Lake Scout Reservation, and other Michigan camps along with our Paul Bunyan Scout Reservation, and Bear Lake Scout Camp (Bear Lake Scout Camp closed under the Lake Huron Area Council period), all had to happen, a sign of the times, so we were told. When Bear Lake Scout Camp closed, I was a member of the Lake Huron Area Council Executive Board at the time, and voted not to sell the property. It was painful to lose prime lake front property that served our youth so well for many years. It's really sad to see camps lock their gates; shut down their buildings, and post no-trespassing signs on their properties. Over the lives of these camps, thousands of scouting volunteers sacrificed, and toiled endlessly making these camps the great camps that they were. The presence of these camps will be missed, but the wonderful memories that they created for us, will forever be with us. RIP, Lost Lake Scout Reservation, Paul Bunyan Scout Reservation, Bear Lake Scout Camp and others.

CHAPTER 6

AROUND THE CAMPFIRE WITH THE WAZ'

Troop 158, sponsored by St. John's Catholic Church, Essexville, MI., at Braden Campsite, week #8 in 2002. Waz' is sitting in his "chair of Honor" that the scouts lashed together for his campfire visit and storytelling. Present in the picture is Tim Jarema, Scoutmaster.

INTRODUCTION

In the scouting circle, I became known as "The Waz." I think someone just shortened my last name way back when. Throughout the years, campers would greet me with, "Hey, Waz, What's up?" And then someone shortened that greeting to "Wazzzuupp?!" And along with the "Wazzzuupp" came the high fives when greeting scouts and scouters. I incorporated the "Wazzzuupp" into a camp-wide cheer. I would yell it to everyone on the parade field, or wherever, and they would yell, repeating it back to me.

The Waz' (that would be I) has been telling tales around campfires for a very long time, and scouts love to hear them. It's been fun catching imaginations with inspirational, and funny stories, and scary ones too. Scouts love to hear tales of all sorts, but mostly they enjoy hearing of ghosts, and of the unknown. I have found that it's a fact; most scouts love to be SCARED! And that is why I picked four of my favorite scary stories that I've been telling for decades. There has been ghostly campfire tales before my tales came along. One of the most popular ghostly figures was Whitey who was the topic of scary stories in the 70's and 80's. Whitey was a real person.

Erv Hutter relates the following: "Whitey was Harold Wilcox, the Camp Ranger from 1960 to 1969. He was known for his white hair, denim jeans, and shirt, and his gruff demeanor. He was the first person employed by the council as a year round caretaker. He lived on Old-27 at Ashard Avenue, just north of the camp entrance on the west side of the road. He had a small gas station at his home, and was the contact person for units visiting camp during the off season. Whitey died on October 17, 1969. Because of his untimely death, Rotary hired a new Ranger, Marv Valentine. Marv developed a number of Whitey stories in his vast repertoire of tales of camp. I spent years cleaning up Whitey's trash piles in camp, which in fact probably weren't just attributed to him, but to a whole different era of how people dealt with getting rid of trash in camp. They just dumped it in the middle of the woods thinking that as long as it wasn't right next to a camp site, then it was fine to dump it there. Most of Whitey's stories I heard came from two sources, staffers Mike Murphy and George Kevin Peshick. Most of the stories are tied to the early years of Central Lodge. Whitey was opposed to the building of Central Lodge, our dining facility, and instead was a strong supporter of the remodeling, and upgrading of the old camp mess hall where the current trading post is now located. He is said to have been camping on the hill where the Central Lodge is, carrying blocks all day for its construction when he suffered his fatal heart attack. His ghost is said to haunt the building. He has been seen "floating" outside the window on the lake side. He has been known to cause havoc in the building by knocking down whole rows of benches off tables, and messing with the lights. He's been heard by various people in the basement of the lodge, and in the kitchen commissary. Of course, this is all bunk. Whitey died in 1969, two years before the construction began on the lodge. I'm sure that he was aware of the plans for the building, at least in concept, because it was part of the capital campaign staged by the Saginaw Bay Area Council which began in 1968. The final plans weren't drawn up until after his death. In fact Marv Valentine had input into those plans, and was the onsite project manager for the council (which by then was Lake Huron Area Council). Whitey may have been against change, his character suggests it, but he was long gone before the change ever happened. Most camps have these kinds of stories, and they for the most part are just harmless bunk-stories that add atmosphere to the place. Murphy and Kevin embellished them with their own weird sense of reality, and I must admit that in the late 70's and early 80's, I passed them on to other staff members who in turn embellished them, and passed them on. Waz's, "The Golden Arm" was even twisted into the lore at one time. My thought is that while these stories have no basis in truth, they were part of the staff landscape."

INTRO TO "THE GOLDEN ARM"

(The first of my Goose-Bump Classics)

I sincerely want to thank the folks who were telling the Whitey tales, back then, paving the way for my tales. I do hope that you enjoy them and if you do; imagine how much more of a scary time you would have, if you were sitting around the campfire with the Waz'.

I heard a ghost story with a very frightening ending (sends everyone out of their seats) in the early 1950's as a young Scout, sitting around a campfire at Camp No-Be-Bos-Co, in Northern Bergen County, New Jersey. Different versions of this tale have been passed-on around the campfire for decades. What I did was incorporate the story's frightening ending into my original storyline. Up to the time that I wrote the John Potter saga; this tale was the granddaddy of all ghost stories. In the tale, I've set the storyline to our local area. One needs to voice the story in low and high tones, and be as dramatic as possible to really capture the audience. The ending comes with an element of surprise, and shock to the listener. Caution, telling this tale before bedtime, you could be staying up part of the night with the scouts. I had to settle a few down insuring them that the tale was fictional, therefore, I would always leave them with a disclaimer at the end, because we just don't need to leave them believing in ghosts. After relating the tale, the "kid in me" would come out too, cause' while walking back to my cabin at night; I would see, and hear unidentified movements in the woods which made me hurry back to my cabin as quickly as I could. Again, up to the time the John Potter came along, this was the most terrifying tale ever told at Rotary.

THE GOLDEN ARM

("Ha-ha! Bet you'll be too scared to sleep tonight").
BY RICH WAZ' WASMER

Anyone hiking up to North Camp along Rotary's northern perimeter will come to what's left of a foundation to an old farmhouse that was once occupied by a farmer, and his wife. You can still see the pieces of cement cinder blocks that formed the foundation embedded in the ground. It's all that remains of the old farmhouse. Some of the locals living on the Clare County road, out by the camp's northern perimeter, claim they hear weird sounds coming from the direction where the old farm house once stood. The sounds were very distinctive and could be heard just after night-fall continuing throughout the early morning hours. They described the sounds as if someone was moaning or someone in distress. They were chilling, and very frightening. As recently as last summer, our Camp Director received a call from a family, outside the perimeter, hearing the sounds. The Camp Director would investigate, but never heard anything himself. But to be safe, he declared North Camp off limits after 11:00 P.M. with no one admitted past Fort Scout camp site, not even Rotary staff. I hate to say, I personally feel sorry for anyone camping at Fort Scott, especially anyone needing to use the newer shower house and latrine after dark. It's located in the Ft. Scott campsite area, just to the south of the boundaries to North Camp. During week number four, in late July of 2005, Troop 103 was camping at Ft. Scott, and one scout had to use the bathroom, and did the unthinkable, he left his tent without his buddy. The number one rule in camp is that NO SCOUT EVER TRAVELS ALONE WITHOUT A BUDDY! But he was lucky; his tent buddy woke up and observed him outside of the tent walking towards the latrine, but he didn't stop at the latrine, he kept going. His tent partner quickly exited and ran after him yelling, "What are you doing? Where are you going, Jason?" Jason didn't reply. His buddy grabbed him by the arm and led him back to their tent. Jason had been sleep-walking. I hate to have imagined what would had happened if his buddy didn't catch up to him, because as they walked their way back, they heard some unexplained, really weird noises in the woods. Another incident occurred during the summer of 2010 when a staff member was told to go the football field in North Camp, and drive the tractor mower back to the Maintenance Building. He was told to do this quickly, taking a buddy with him and get back pronto. It was dark as he headed out to North Camp on foot, but, (DAH!) without a buddy. The moon was a full one, and he could see most of his surroundings without a flashlight. While on the road, he kept hearing strange noises, and saw movements in the brush. "It must be a deer or some wild turkeys," he thought to himself. He didn't give it any further thought when a buck ran right in front of his path. But it almost made him pee in pants. When he got to the football field and the tractor, he again sensed a movement in the woods. "Must be that same deer," He muttered. But then he heard sounds, moaning sounds. He quickly jumped on the tractor, turn the ignition key and like most of the motored equipment in camp, it wouldn't start. Sitting on the tractor, the moaning, and movement seem to be closer; anxiety had kicked in as he kept turning the key trying to get the tractor started. He didn't know who or what was making the sound, and he didn't want to find out. "I should have taken a buddy with me," He told himself. Along with the movements and sounds, he now heard footsteps and they seem to be really close. He found the manual choke to the tractor, and turned the ignition key again, and was praying that it would turn over, because he just wanted out of there. By now he was very frightened, and the sweat was running down his back as the sounds kept coming closer in his direction. Finally, the motor kicked in, and was he relieved as he pressed his foot to accelerate, gassing it like a race car driver in the Indy 500, leaving that football field as fast as he could, never looking back. The next day he told the Program Director what he had experienced. The Program Director replied, "Oh, you just heard a bear." The staffer replied, "It was no bear, I tell you, it was something that sounded eerie and evil." He was right because he came very close to an encounter with the unknown.

I need to go back now, to the property, and farm house, years ago when it was a striving productive farm. A husband and wife team ran the farm which consisted of many acres of planting and harvesting, mainly corn. The husband and wife toiled long hours from sunrise to sunset, seven days a week. They had no children, and to say that their marriage was not a happy one was an understatement. They actually despised each other. Before they met, the wife inherited much wealth from an uncle, and placed much of it into the farm that she managed herself. She was growing older, and was known as a rich old maid, a title that she did not appreciate. She hired an extra hand who eventually became her husband, and whose work ethics were very good. They seem to be very close at first. She thought she knew him well, and that he loved her. However, his reason for marriage was much different than hers. She was very rich and he was poor. Once married, he thought that he would live life in grand style. The problem was, she was very stingy with her money, and would spend it only on the bare necessities in operating the farm. She seldom gave him anything. He resented this, and they would often argue and actually fought at times. It didn't take long before she realized that he did not care for her at all. He had married her, not out of love, but out of greed. Over time, she grew to resent him. There was no trust between them, which made their work days even longer as they hardly spoke to each other.

One unfaithful day, while the wife was working driving the farm tractor, in the corn field, she approached some uneven terrain near a ditch. She lost control and the tractor tilted sideways with her falling to the ground. The tractor followed her fall, and landed on her. Passed out, she laid by the ditch for hours before her husband found her. He freed her from the fallen tractor, and carried her to the barn placing her in the back of the horse and buggy, and started the long ride to the hospital. There he just dropped her off telling the doctors what had happened and that he had to get back to the farm to finish his chores. The hospital staff couldn't believe what they were hearing, "His chores were more important than his wife?"

His wife lay unconscious in a coma for five days: when she finally awoke in her hospital bed, she gave out a loud scream. She noticed that on her left side she had no arm, it had been amputated. Gangrene had set in leaving the doctors no choice. She was very depressed and angry; angry mostly at her husband, "Who just dropped me off," she said, "One week in the hospital and he never visited." She was disorientated some, and confused from all the medication that she was on. Crazy thoughts ran through her head. She summoned her lawyer, and told him what she wanted done, and informed the doctors what they were to do. The doctors didn't think she was in the right frame of mine, but her lawyer told them they had no choice; her wishes were to be carried out. The lawyer withdrew all her wealth from the bank, and purchased pure gold, and then had the gold melted down, and poured into a mold of an artificial limb, an arm, which the doctors attached to her left shoulder. Her husband never loved her; he married her only for her money, and this was her way to get even with him for the loveless life that they shared.

After 10 days in the hospital her husband finally came to see her, and when he found out what she had done, he was furious. He couldn't believe she had accomplished such a deed. Back on the farm, their lives together were worse than before; there was absolutely no interaction and very little verbal contact between them. It was a marriage from hell. Her wealth was gone; he was a broken man with nothing to live for. So he thought at the time. Late one night, he awoke from a sound sleep steering at the bedroom window. It was a clear night with a full moon. He heard a coyote barking from a distance. He could hear his wife, sound asleep in her bedroom snoring very loudly. "Wait," he thought to himself, "Why am I living like this? It's true that she emptied her bank account and all the cash is gone. But there's gold and plenty of it. Yes, gold in the form of an arm. That gold, rightfully, belongs to me!" He continued, "That gold is mine and only mine. I had to put up and live with the old witch and her bickering all these years." He snickered to himself: with half of a grin devised a plan, a hideous and evil one. He was going to get rid of the only thing standing in his way from being rich. He was going to kill his wife.

His plan had to be a perfect one. He didn't want any suspicion coming his way; he had to make it look like an accident. It was to be a perfect homicide. Weeks went by: all he could think about was his plan. He kept going over, and over it in every detail until he was ready to make his move. One evening, upstairs in his bedroom of the farmhouse, he kept his ear peeled to his closed door listening for his wife's footsteps climbing the stairwell. He heard her them, and when they got to the top of the stairs, he quickly opened his door, gave a terrifying yell, ran over to her, and with both hands extended, pushed her sending her tumbling down the stairwell. His eyes focused on the motionless body at the bottom of the steps. He approached the body; it was still. Her eyes were opened wide. He checked her pulse; there wasn't any. He closed her eyes lids, and smiled yelling out "YES!" He had accomplished his evil deed.

After tidying things up, he notified the police that there had been a terrible accident; his wife had fallen. When the ambulance arrived, followed by law enforcement, he put on a very convincing, remorseful act that could have earned him an academy award. All throughout the interview with the police, he cried. To the police, it looked indeed like a tragic accident. He wife had fallen, and broken her neck. Mentally, he patted himself on the back for his performance in executing a perfect murder. His thought process told him everything would work out exactly as he had planned it.

A few days later, at the funeral home, he continued his academy award performance. He cried and cried expressing much sorrow. Everyone felt much grief for his loss. And at the cemetery, as they placed her body in the ground, and while the minister recited, "Ashes to ashes, dust to dust," he was saying to himself, "And the golden arm for me." The cemetery was in close proximity to his farm, and that was an important part of the second segment to his plan, because his next move was to be a horrifying one. It was late in the evening, the day after the funeral; a peaceful night, very warm. You could hear a train in the distance along with some dogs barking. And if you were close enough, you could hear the sound of a shovel digging out a newly closed grave. The husband was at his wife's grave site working frantically shoveling dirt from her grave. He was very tired, and weary, but the thought of the gold kept him forging on. His mind wasn't right. I mean what kind of a human being would be out in a graveyard after committing such an unforgiven sin. He kept spading, and throwing the dirt up top, and alongside the grave. He worked for hours until his spade hit something solid. He had reached his target, the top of his wife's coffin. He quickly cleared the dirt, and with the shovel, pried the top of the coffin opened. Raising the lid, his eyes were fixed to his wife's corpse. Her color was a greenish blue. "Wait, what's that," he cried out. He could have sworn that his dead wife blinked at him. The sight of her golden arm at her side caused him to give out a hideous laugh. With a knife, he carefully carved away at her shoulder separating the golden arm from her body. He wrapped his treasure in a large piece of cloth, and threw it to the top of the grave. He closed the coffin, and as fast as he could shovel the dirt back into the hole. He replaced the fresh flowers on the top of the grave. He did this very carefully having it look like the grave was never disturbed.

Back at the farm house, he carried the cloth with the golden arm upstairs to his bedroom, and placed the creepy thing in his dresser drawer. He cleaned up and went to bed. He couldn't sleep too well. He thought about all that he had accomplished. "I'm the perfect criminal," he said to himself as he tried to doze off. In the morning, he tended to his farm duties thinking back to the cemetery and how his wife appeared lying in the coffin. It freaked him out especially when he thought she was winking at him. Now that he had the gold, he would have to make plans to go somewhere and get cash for that golden limb. He didn't want to make himself look suspicious to anyone because every now and then a neighbor would drop by and lend him support. So he continued to work the farm trying to make everything appear as normal as possible. A few days went by and he decided to wait another day before he would just disappear from the scene, leaving the farm intact, then travel somewhere out of state, and cash in his wife's arm. He had to do it sooner than later because he was finding it more difficult to sleep at night. Every evening, he heard unexplained noises coming from outside the farm house.

It was about 11:00 P.M., and he went upstairs to his bedroom ready for sleep. His mind was racing; all he could think about was getting away from the farm. With the help of some medication, he fell asleep. At 3 A.M. he was aroused from his sleep by an eerie sound coming from the outside. Sitting up in bed, he pounded, "What was that?" It was kind of a high pitch sound, almost like a human voice, but then again it didn't sound human at all. It was almost like someone was calling for help. After several minutes the noise went away. He lay back down thinking to himself, "I got to get away. I'll give it another day, and it won't be soon enough. I got to get hold of my sanity." He fell asleep again. Outside of the farm house the sound returned, but it wasn't loud enough to wake him. The sound was definitely coming from the direction of the cemetery.

Morning came, and it was to be his last full day on the farm. He had a hard time completing his daily chores because of a headache that came and went. "Probably from a lack of sleep," he thought to himself. On this day he packed some suitcases, and finalized his plans to leave early the next day; never to return again. He had mailed a letter to a distant cousin saying that he had to leave unexpectedly for a job prospect, and asked him to watch over the farm, and that he would be in touch. Evening came and dinner; he went upstairs to his bedroom having one more thing to pack. Opening the dresser drawer, he took out the golden arm, and placed it in one of the suit cases.

His headache was still present. He took some pills, and laid on the bed closing his eyes. He fell asleep, but not for long. He woke up, and sitting up in his bed heard the noises again. This time the sounds were clearer, and sounded very, very close. OOOOOOOHHH, CAME FROM THE OUTSIDE OF THE HOUSE. THE OOOOOOHHH SOUNDED LIKE SOMEONE OR SOMETHING WAS MOANING AND IT WAS LOUDER THAN EVER. He got up; opened his bedroom window, looked down towards the front steps of the house. He was scared, but what terrified him next, were the footsteps he heard. He could hear footsteps climbing the front steps. He ran back to bed covering his head, and blurted out, "I'm losing my mind, I can't take it anymore. Someone's trying to scare me." He got up from bed, and grabbed his 12-gauge shotgun from the closet. Unlatched the safety, and jumped back in bed covering his head again. He thought he heard the front door to the house open. Oh no! The moaning sound sounded like it was in the house. "OOOOOOHHH," and along with the noise came the footsteps, climbing the stairwell to his bedroom. Holding his loaded 12-gauge close to his chest, and with his head covered with the blanket, he closed his eyes thinking he might pass out. "OOOOOOHHH" AND THE FOOTSTEPS NOW WERE CLIMBING THE STAIRS. He couldn't utter a word. He was shaking, and perspiring as the footsteps, "OOOOOOOHHH" were now just outside his bedroom door. Crutching the shotgun under the blanket and aiming with trembling hands towards the bedroom door, he heard the door open. His whole bed was shaking as the horrifying sound and footsteps were now in the bedroom. He wanted to release the trigger to the gun but his fingers would not move. Closer to his bed came the footsteps, and the sounds which were clearer than ever, OOOOOHHH, WHO STOLE MY GOLDEN ARM, OOOOHH. OOOOOHHH, WHO STOLE MY GOLDEN ARM? OOOOHHH! He was completely numbed. The ghostly sound came from a familiar voice; the voice of his dead wife. WHO STOLE MY GOLDEN ARM, WHO STOLE MY GOLDEN ARM, WHO STOLE MY GOLDEN ARM?

"DID YOU?!!!!!!!!"

AUTHOR'S NOTE: I would be walking around the campfire, and in low tones, repeat three or more times, "Who stole my golden arm?"

When I was really close to a bunch of un-expecting sitting scouts, yell out as loud as I could

"DID YOU?!!!!"

Believe me; the way you relate this story can be very effective. From the beginning of the story to its end, I had them in my grasp with the ending scaring the heck out of them. It's a proven. The scouts love it. I added my disclaimer at the end. Man, I had fun with this one over the years.

THE COFFIN

A GOOSEBUMP TALE
BY RICH WAZ' WASMER

INTRODUCTION

I authored this story back in 1996. Believe it or not, the title came from a joke that I heard years ago. So, I came up with this scary story line which precedes the joke. I tried not to make it too scary, suitable to tell everyone, even the first year scouts. Like all scouts, they too enjoy hearing about ghosts, but I couldn't include them in on the "John Potter" story. It was just too terrifying. So I had to come up with another story, and the "Coffin," which ended with a humorous punch line, was a good fit for everyone. It's what I call an official goose bump story. Over the years, many have heard it in their campsites, and on the P.A.T.H. over-night encampment. In this lighter version of a scary story, I would inform the listeners that it would be a little scary throughout, but the ending was not. I didn't want them leaving before the punch line. Unlike the adults, many of the younger scouts never did get the jest of the ending, because they were too absorbed in believing the story actually happened. Many would ask, "What happened to the scouts (in the story) and were they okay? Imaginations can run wild. For many, it's difficult in separating reality from fabrication. I would walk around the campfire, walking stick in hand, and with my campaign hat on; in my story telling-mode, tell the tale. I had their attention.

THE COFFIN

It was in 1924 when the property of Camp Rotary was bought by the Rotary Club of Saginaw, and leased to the local scout council for their summer camp which opened to campers in 1925. This is the story of three Boy Scouts from Saginaw, Michigan who were curious to see what the property looked like. So, they decided to spend a fall weekend in October of 1924, and get a preview of their new summer camp. With their backpacks, they boarded a train, early in the morning hours, in Saginaw, and railed it to Clare. The train ride took 5 hours before finally arriving at the depot in down town Clare. From the down town area they hiked, with map in hand, the 8 miles on U.S. 27 (just a dirt road at the time) to the main gate of Rotary. Along the route they saw tall pine trees with thick underbrush, and much wild life. Clare County, in those days, was primitive compared to today and so was the camp's property. Rotary had only one building, no electricity; just beautiful Beebe Lake, and hills with lots of trees. The forest land was much thicker than today. The Scout Council had hired a Camp Ranger, who with some local contractors started the foundation to a dining hall, and camp office, where the trading post is located today. The Ranger also set up markers for Rotary's different campsites. On this particular October weekend, the property was deserted with no one in camp except for an old man. While walking to the camp gate onto the camp property, these three scouts met the old guy as he was walking out of camp. The old guy carried a fishing pole over his shoulder, and on the pole were the biggest trophy size fish that these scouts have ever seen. The old man stopped and talked with the scouts saying, "You boys camping at Rotary this weekend?" The boys were frozen in their tracks eyeing those big fish. They have never seen fish like these. Luckily they had brought along their fishing poles. One of the Scouts spoke up, "Yeah, mister, we just want to see what camp is like." "Well, boys, this is a beautiful piece of property, and you'll going to love your new scout camp." He continued, "And as you can see, the fish are really biting in Beebe Lake. So, if I were you three, I'd set up your camp by the lake, and have lots of fun with the fish." He went on, "But, let me caution you, whatever you do, do not, just don't camp over there," as he pointed towards Curtis Campsite. "Why not," one of the scouts spoke up. He replied, "Well, boys, there's an old house standing close by that campsite, and the locals around here think it is haunted. They claim to hear strange noises coming from the house at night, like screams. Why, a few years back, an old hermit walked into the old house, and he never did come back out. For months the Clare County Sheriff's Department, and other folks looked for him in that house. They never did find him." The scouts just stood there with their dropped jaws not believing what they were hearing. The old man started walking out towards the gate: from a distance, he turned, yelled in their direction, "Remember to stay clear of Curtis. It's no place for boys like you. Remember!"

The scouts still steadfast in their tracks looked at the old man as he turned, and disappeared onto the main road. The scouts did an about-face towards the direction of Beebe Lake running as fast as they could to the lake front. There, they dropped their back packs; grabbed their fishing rods, and started casting. Sure enough, they began catching the big ones. The fish came really fast and plentiful. They were having so much fun, but the fun had worn down, for now it was getting kind of boring with all those fish. The sun was about to set and the evening would soon be upon them. They had scores of fish, and had to prepare a fire to cook them. One of the scouts looked at the other two and said, "What did you think of that old guy telling us that tale of his?" One of the other scouts replied, "I think he was crazy. He was just an old kook who wanted to scare us." The third scout agreed, "Yeah, who can believe a nutty old man like that telling us about ghosts, and things. We're scouts, and scouts are brave, and don't believe in ghosts. You, know, guys, what would really be fun? We've gone on lots of campouts. We have had polar bear campouts; orienteering campouts, and pioneering campouts. But we never have had a haunted house campout. Wouldn't that be fun?" They all agreed it would be, and looking at their camp map, defying the old man's warning, they picked up their gear heading to Curtis Campsite.

At Curtis, they set up their camp, made a nice campfire, and cooked their fish. It was a beautiful evening with some dynamic star formations. The scouts, years ago were no different than scouts today. After eating they sat around their campfire singing songs, and roasting marshmallows while telling jokes. But this camp fire in this campsite was a whole lot different than anyone they've ever experienced before. Because every now and then, one of the scouts would turn on his flash light, and aim the beam about 50 yards away towards the haunted house. It was a creepy building but these scouts were not afraid, and determined to prove to themselves and anyone that they could survive the night on their haunted house campout.

At the campfire, one of the scouts spoke up, "You know, I bet I could go into that house, and never be scared." "Bet you can't," came the reply from one of the other scouts, "Bet you wouldn't even last 5 minutes and you'd run out screaming." "I would not," he flashed back, quickly. He was embarrassed, wanting to prove his bravery. With the "I'll show them" attitude, he picked up his flashlight, and walked towards the haunted house leaving his unbelieving buddies at the campfire. His buddies watched him as he climbed the steps to the haunted house. They watched him as he opened the front door, and disappeared inside with the door closing behind him. The haunted house had some very large windows, and the scouts at the campfire couldn't actually see their buddy, but he had his flashlight on, and they could see his shadow moving about. 3 minutes passed, 4 minutes and then at 5 minutes, and then the beam from the flashlight went out. "Okay, you won the bet," one of the scouts yelled towards the house. No answer came back. 7 minutes passed and then 10 minutes. This time both scouts yelled towards the house, but still no response. "I bet he's pulling a trick on us," the scout said to the other, then hesitating, "Or maybe he had an accident, or fell, or something." The other scout said, "Maybe one of us should go in and find out." "I'll go," the other scout said, "and you stay here at the fire, I'll go in and find out, but I know he just wants to scare us." So the scout took his flashlight while leaving the lone scout at the fire, he started to the porch of the house. The lone scout watched as his friend opened the front door, and went inside. The lone scout could not see him inside, but could see the beam from the flashlight moving about. 5 minutes passed, and then 8 and 10 minutes and then the light went out! The lone scout at the campfire yelled out, "Did you see anything?" There was no response. He asked himself "Why are they trying to scare me like this?" He didn't want to admit it, but he had stored up some anxiety over the situation. Sure he was scared, but he was a brave kid, and although he didn't believe in ghosts, he was having second thoughts, now. "Okay," he shouted, "I'm coming in and you two are going to be sorry that you're doing this to me." He took his flashlight, and headed towards the house. Climbing the porch steps, he reached the front door. He turned the door knob, and stepped inside the home, and once inside, the door slammed shut, on its own, behind him. He gave out such a loud yell that he even startled himself. With his light on, he noticed that he must have been in the living room. There was a large couch in the center of the room with cobwebs in every corner. The drapes over the windows were torn, and stained. There were some old portraits on the wall. He shined his light away from the living room area into what looked like a long narrow hallway. He thought he heard noises coming from the end of the hallway. Very slowly he made his way down the long hallway;

he was shaking in his shoes. He came upon a closed door, and the noises were coming from behind the door. "They must be in there trying to scare me," half assuring himself. Very cautiously he opened the door, and found it very dark inside. He shined his light towards his feet, and discovered that he was the top of a stairwell, steps leading to the basement of the haunted house. He shouted, "I know you guys are down there, I can hear you!" He continued, "I'm coming down and you two are going to be sorry!" Very slowly he started down those steps, taking one at a time. He reached the bottom. He shined his light on all four walls of the basement, and on one wall, there appeared to be a long object lying on the floor. He heard noises coming from that object, whatever it was. He walked with short steps towards it, and the closer he got; the more he became focused on what he was seeing. That long object was a COFFIN! A coffin, lying on the floor. There were noises coming from within the coffin. He thought to himself, "I just know these guys are playing a trick on me." He was only a foot from the coffin when he took his flashlight, and rapped on it as hard as he could. You won't believe what happened next? That coffin on its own stood up, on its end, in the upright position. It startled him so much that he flew backwards to the ground with his flashlight flying from his hand. As he sat there on the basement floor, he caught his breath, and gave out a very loud shrieking yell. Then you won't believe what occurred next. The coffin, standing on its end, started inching itself, in the upright position, coming towards him. He kept sliding backwards on the seat of his pants. He kept moving backwards with the coffin following. He was so scared, he thought he'd wet his pants. He kept sliding, and sliding with the coffin only inches away. Then he could move no more. On the seat of his pants, he felt his back pressing against the basement wall. His flashlight was out of reach, but he knew he had to do something, and do something quickly. He felt in his pants pocket looking for his trusted Boy Scout knife. He was looking for anything that could help him get out of this horrifying situation. He remembered that he left his knife outside at the campfire when he was whittling a marshmallow stick. The coffin was oh-so close, and it looked like the cover to the coffin was opening as the voices inside became terribly loud. He was sweating, and still reaching into his pockets trying to find something; anything. He felt something in his pants that seem to be a small square object. He pulled it out of his pants pocket, it was a little box wrapped in cellophane. The coffin was directly over him, and the cover was almost completely opened exposing a figure of something so hideous and indescribable. With that little square box in hand, he tore the cellophane off, and opened the box, and felt what he thought was some little hard candies on the inside. He grabbed some of those hard little drops placing them in his mouth, one after another, and sucked on them as quickly as he could with its juices, rapidly, running down his throat. The top of the coffin was now completely opened and a slimy big HAIRY ARM AND HAND with long sharp POINTED FINGER NAILS reached out towards him, he gave out the most terrifying scream ever AAAAAHHHHHH!! OMG!!!!! He feared the worse was upon him FOR HE NOW BELIEVED IN GHOST!!! OMG!!!....BUT DID HE WORRY?

NO! YOU SEE, SCOUTS, THAT LITTLE BOX, IN HIS HAND, WAS FILLED WITH COUGH DROPS, AND WITH THOSE COUGH DROPS THAT HE SUCKED ON, HE STOPPED THE "COFFIN."

GHOST BUDDY
ANOTHER GOOSEBUMP CAMPFIRE TALE

BY RICH "WAZ" WASMER

INTRODUCTION

This story was written well over 30 years ago. The idea, and then words just came to me, and I rapidly put it all together on paper. Part of the story is factual with actual occurrences while some parts are not. At the end of the tale, just about everyone leaves the campfire stunned. It's creepy, believable, and very captive to an audience. Between 1958 and 1961, I was in the United States Air Force stationed in Spain. My home duty station was in Northern Spain close to the little town (pueblo) of "La Muela," The translation, I'm told, means "The Tooth." My duty station was a military fuel storage site, located on top of a mountain area, This was a great duty for it gave me the opportunity to travel throughout Spain (Espana) maintaining a pipeline operated by the U.S. Air Force that supplied aviation, jet and diesel fuel to the different Air Bases at Rota, Seville, Madrid and Zaragoza. There were also pipeline booster sites between these bases that I worked. Notice that I mentioned Air Bases, and not Air Force Bases. The Spanish government, under Dictator General Franco mandated that the word "Force" not be indicated. Also as a point of interest, our American Flag could not be raised first to the top of the flag pole. It had to follow the Spanish Flag. Spain is a wonderful country with wonderful citizens, and there's so much to see. Sightseeing was my top priority, because every town and city had its unique sights with much history, from gigantic and elegant cathedrals to Roman, and Moorish ruins, and standing castles from centuries ago. The country has many celebrations or fiestas. Bull fights are a spectacular form of entertainment, and centered to most of the fiestas. I would visit as many fiestas as possible; the most awesome and exciting was in Pamplona with the running of the bulls. I'm told that Pamplona was where Ernest Hemmingway stayed, and authored one of his books.

I arrived in Spain on Veterans Day, November 11, 1958. I was a young airman, only 19 years old at the time. I had taken Spanish in high school, so I was looking forward to this tour of duty, and I quickly began to appreciate everything about it. I found the country, and its culture, and especially the cuisine to be a wonderful experience. Dinner time in Spain was typically around 2200 Hrs. (10 P.M.) in the evening which was hard for me to get accustomed to. Most everything seems to stop in mid-afternoon when stores and shops would close for two or three hours for the daily siesta (rest period).

When I wasn't on duty, I'd be visiting as much of the country as possible. I stayed as busy as possible because, frankly when Idle, I would feel lonely being so far from home. Home was in New Jersey with over three thousand miles of ocean separating myself from Mom and Dad. So, I chose to stay occupied. I even traveled outside of Spain to Germany, Portugal, The Azores, Scotland, France, Luxemburg, Gibraltar and North Africa. I was an Assistant Scoutmaster with troop 328 and a member of the Black Eagle OA Lodge (Transatlantic Council) at Zaragoza Air Base. The troop camped throughout much of Europe and North Africa. Most of the scouts were in Little League Sanction ball and in the summer of 1960, I helped with the All-Star team from the base. We won the Spain and North African Championships, and went to Bonn, Germany for the European Play-offs. In Bonn, we beat Little League all-star teams from England, and Turkey and made it to the finals where Germany defeated us, three to two. My team was devastated. There wasn't a dry eye anywhere. We had worked so hard to get to where we were; just one game from going to Williamsport, Pa., for the Little League World Series. TWA flew the Germany team to Williamsport where they lost all their games in the playoffs.

GHOST BUDDY

It was during the Christmas holidays in 1960 that an unbelievable, chilling event occurred. An out-of-the "Tri-Light Zone" happening that still takes my breath away to this day.

The following is a true story. While I was a young airman with the United States Air Force, stationed in the country of Spain, an event happened that questioned my sanity at the time. It was so bizarre, and an experience that I'll never put aside. It was during the Christmas Holidays in 1960 that I, and two of my close Air Force chums decided to spend a short vacation on a beautiful Island belonging to Spain. The Island of Majorca, located in the Mediterranean Sea, and the largest of a series of Islands in the Balearic Island chain. It is an extremely popular and beautiful tourist designation for many Europeans. Both of my friends hailed from upper New York State, and since I was from New Jersey, we hit it off well, and bonded throughout our tour in Spain. Since the Christmas season was somewhat weary on us, being so far from homes, we thought that a change of scenery would get us through the holidays easier.

It was on the 22nd of December 1960 that we boarded a train from Zaragoza to Madrid, and then another one to Barcelona. From Barcelona we boarded an old German aircraft. Old is an understatement. The pilot had to start the aircraft manually using a hand crank located at the nose of the aircraft. I was told during W.W.II; General Franco was an ally to Hitler. Germany supplied Spain with its planes for Spain's Air Force. The flight only took 20 minutes, and we landed in Majorca's capitol, Palma; truly a tropical paradise with palm trees covering the Island. The temperature averaged between 70 and 80 degrees with plenty of sun year round. There was so much to do on the Island. After checking into our hotel, we rented a car, and went sightseeing. The streets in Palma are very narrow and the roadways are made of cobblestone, centuries old. There were unique restaurants; all of international flare serving great food. We decided to use the hotel pool and later do some water skiing in the bay. It was a Christmas vacation of doing lots of fun things.

It was in the early evening of December 24th, Christmas Eve; we were at a great French restaurant enjoying a great meal. Christmas day was approaching, and I started feeling sorry for myself. I kept day dreaming of the holidays at home as a youth with the family. I told my two friends that I was going back to the hotel. They recognized my despair. They mentioned that I should go with them to the local night spot that we had visited the night before. It would cheer me up. I rejected the idea. I just wanted to be alone. I left them, and started back to the hotel walking the long narrow roadways through the city. I stopped at a local pub, sat at a table, ordered a drink; I was really feeling down. It was midnight and Christmas day had arrived. All of a sudden, from behind, a hand landed on my shoulder. It startled me. I turned to see who it was. The person who touched me had a familiar face and said, "Hi, Waz." I was shocked to see a home town buddy of mine. Jacob Rabidue. Jake and I attended school together from kindergarten through high school. We played varsity football and baseball, and even worked at the same grocery store chain. We both dated the same set of twin sisters, Barbara and Cindy, and went on many dates together. I couldn't believe my eyes. Here I am sitting in a pub on a little island over three thousand miles from home, feeling depressed, and an old buddy appears from nowhere. We hugged and talked, and we chatted about everything, especially all the fun stuff we did together over the years. It was three years prior to this encounter, that we both had entered the Arm Forces, Jake enlisted in the Army and me in the Air force. The hours ticked on by and it was around 0200 hours when it finally dawned on me to ask Jacob what he was doing on this tiny little island. "Jake," I questioned, "The last I knew you were deployed somewhere in Asia." He replied, "Yeah, Waz I was. But I'm here to give you this." He placed some money on the table. "Jake," I spurted out, what's this for?" "Waz, he replied, "Remember the time on our senior prom together with Barb and Cindy, I got my wallet ripped off, and you loaned me funds to get through one of the most enjoyable events in my life?" I replied, "Jake, I completely forgot, and I don't want your money. Just being here, you've made my Christmas, I felt so lonely before seeing you." I mentioned to him to stay put at the table. I needed to go use the restroom, and we had much to catch up on. As I got up to leave the table, he stood up with me. He grabbed my arm and gave me one of our famous football games' hugs that we used to exchange with each other. I was so excited. When I got back to the table, Jake wasn't there. I asked the bartender where he went. "What guy," he replied with a puzzled look on his face that puzzled me even more. There was a hand written note lying on the table. It read, "Waz, thanks for the friendship throughout the years. I'm sorry I had to leave like this, I had no choice, but I promise we'll see each other again at the wall." I couldn't believe this was happening. I left the pub and ran down those narrow little streets looking for him. It was in the wee hours of the morning and I didn't see him anywhere. Just as mysteriously as Jacob appeared, he disappeared. I searched for long time. It was turning daylight and I headed to the hotel. My two buddies were fast asleep. I collapsed on the bed having a hard time getting to sleep, thinking back to the pub and the note Jacob had written. What did he mean, "I had no choice and that he'll see me at the wall?" It absolutely made no sense.

My two friends were ready, and roaring to go around 0900 Hrs., and wanted to do a full day of activities because it was our last day on the Island. They asked me how my night went. I told them the whole episode. They sat in their bunks in disbelief thinking I had too much to drink. Throughout the last day on the Island, I tried to join in the fun but couldn't get motivated. Wherever we went, I kept looking over my shoulder in hopes of spotting Jacob. But never did. The following day, we flew back to Barcelona and the mainland.

It was in the 4th week of January 1961 on a Saturday. I was back at the Air Base in Zaragoza performing CQ (Charge of Quarters) duty. My responsibilities were to watch over everything pertaining to the barracks, and personnel, over a twenty four hour period. I would have to man the phones, and in cases of rare emergencies, take appropriate actions. It was in the early morning hours, and many of the tenants were out on week-end passes. So it was very slow, hardly anyone was around, the phones were silent. In the last four weeks all that I could think about was my chance meeting with Jacob in Palma. Did I imagine it all? No, it was real, and I wouldn't let it go. I went to the Day Room which is a place for us Airmen to go, and relax. There's a pop, and snack machine in the Day Room along with a refrigerator, pool table, and ping pong tables, and T.V. I grabbed a coke and sat down on the sofa next to a magazine rack. The Arm Forces Network was about to sign off on the T.V. The current episode of "Gunsmoke" had just aired. I grabbed a magazine not looking at its title; I started thumbing through the pages. I noticed pictures of people, men and women with captions below their photos. The sizes of the photographs were like you'd see in a high school year book of underclassmen. This was a thick issue with only the photos, and captions filing the many pages. I quickly closed the magazine and peered at the front cover. It was a special edition of "Life" dated January 1961. The title of his special issue read "Viet Nam War Casualties." There were many, many photos; all casualties from the Viet Nam Conflict. I kept turning the pages, one after another looking at all those military heroes when I came upon a face that I had seen recently. "No. It can't be!" I shouted. My eyes were fixed and focused, but my brain didn't want to register what I was seeing. I could hardly catch my breath as the panic raced within me. My eyes turned down to the caption below the photo. It read, "Private Jacob Rabidue, United States Army; killed in action, Da Nang, Viet Nam, December 24, 1960." I wanted to pass out.

I just can't explain the happenings of the Christmas day on that little Island in the Mediterranean. I just know the events of that day happened. There is a plague on a small boulder in a park with Jacob's name on it, back in our hometown in Jersey. Jake was killed by enemy gun fire on his SECOND tour of duty to Nam, a second tour which he volunteered for.

After my tour in Spain, I re-enlisted, and was sent to a base in Michigan. I spent four years there; met and married a wonderful girl. In August of 1966 I was honorably discharged' residing in Bay City, Michigan. I found employment at the huge Dow Chemical complex in Midland. We raised a family. The years went by. Although life had its ups, and downs, it was basically good. In 1997, the wife and I decided to take a trip to Washington, D.C. We visited many memorials and there was a newer one, erected in 1982, that I was particularly interested in; the Viet Nam Memorial. Walking down the walk way alongside this long memorial with more than 50,000 names, all casualties of the conflict, I was focused only on one thing. I found Jacob's name engraved on this magnificent piece of graphite. I was beside myself with emotion, and on the brink of tears. I took my trembling hand, and with my fingertips went back and forth covering the engraving. I did this for several minutes, then, from behind, I felt someone placing his hand on my shoulder, just like someone had done on that Christmas Eve, 37 years ago. I completely froze. I did not turn around to see who it was. I half wanted to, but didn't. Chills ran down my back as the tears started to flow. Then after a time, the hand left me. I backed away from the monument, and walked away, down the walkway, never looking back. I just couldn't look back. You see, I wanted to believe it was Jacob's hand that I felt, on my shoulder, as he fulfilled his promise in seeing me again at the "Wall."

Authors Note: Although much of the preceding story is fiction, our men and women serving in our Armed Services and our Veterans are NOT. Many of our scouts and scouters are serving in the military, and many are veterans. I recently heard from Adam Jerema. "AJ" who was a member of troop 158 from Essexville, Michigan, and served as a C.I.T. at Rotary, has a leadership role with the U.S. Army stationed overseas. Former Camp Rotary staffer and member of Troop 108 in Bay City, Andrew Comtois, served in the United States Marine Corps. Andrew was honorably discharged from active service, but continues to serve his country in the Marine Corps Reserves. Lieutenant Brandon Knox, a graduate of the U.S. Naval Academy, and now a Navy fighter pilot was a C.I.T. at Rotary. A former member of Troop 121 in Bay City, I was honored to be named as his "Mentor" at his Eagle ceremony. Thank you Brandon, "AJ" and Andrew for your service to our Country. Please remember all of our scouts and scouters and others, our men and women who have served, and are serving in our Armed Forces in your thoughts and prayers, especially those HEROS who have given the supreme sacrifice.

CHAPTER 7

CAMP ROTARY'S JOHN, THE HANNIBAL, POTTER

BY RICH 'WAZ' WASMER
THE SCARIEST CAMP TALE EVER!

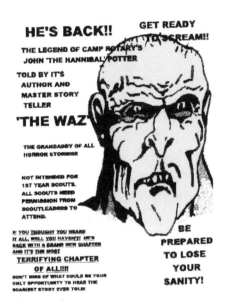

HE'S BACK!! GET READY TO SCREAM!!

THE LEGEND OF CAMP ROTARY'S
JOHN 'THE HANNIBAL' POTTER

TOLD BY IT'S
AUTHOR AND
MASTER STORY
TELLER

'THE WAZ'

THE GRANDADDY OF ALL
HORROR STORIES!!

NOT INTENDED FOR
1ST YEAR SCOUTS.
ALL SCOUTS NEED
PERMISSION FROM
SCOUTLEADERS TO
ATTEND.

IF YOU THOUGHT YOU HEARD
IT ALL, WELL YOU HAVEN'T! HE'S
BACK WITH A BRAND NEW CHAPTER
AND IT'S THE MOST
**TERRIFYING CHAPTER
OF ALL!!!!**
DON'T MISS OF WHAT COULD BE YOUR
ONLY OPPORTUNITY TO HEAR THE
SCARIEST STORY EVER TOLD!

BE
PREPARED
TO LOSE
YOUR
SANITY!

INTRODUCTION

The main reason in writing "Whenever Rotary Scouts Fall in Line" is this very story. I began writing this tale in 1997, and a year later finished it. Thousands of scouts and leaders have heard it, and they requested this horror of all horror stories in a book form from the on start. Over the years, there have been ghost or horror stories of all sorts told in camp, but none ever came close to this terrifying saga. I first showed the story to Staffer Dan Tanciar, who was the "Camp's Office Person" at the time, and his immediate response was, "Waz, you're not really going to tell this to scouts, are you?" John Potter isn't just the run-of-the-mill horror story that gives everyone goose bumps. It is a terrifying tale leaving the listener, to different degrees, really shaken up. Ron Comtois, long-time Scoutmaster, from Troop 108 in Bay City, said he was up all night long in Curtis campsite trying to settle his scouts down after they heard it. I've received similar comments from other scout leaders. As with any fictional tale, scary or not, I place a disclaimer at the end saying the story was not true, it was from my imagination, and there was nothing to fear. Would you believe that the scouts didn't want to hear the disclaimer; they wanted to believe the story was factual. But a disclaimer is appropriate, and a necessity, especially with youth protection in place. We don't want the story to be labeled as a form of hazing. I marketed the tale extremely well throughout each camp week because I had between 50 to 150 or more scouts, and leaders that showed up for the tale. I would tell the story at a different campsite each week. During summer camp, week six in 2012, the attendance broke an all-time record with 320 in attendance at Fretwell Campsite hosted by a Garden City, Michigan troop. Some scouts would leave the story during the introduction which set the mood on how terrifying the tale was going to be. Some left in the beginning or middle of the story, and that was okay as I encouraged them to do so. During my marketing, I gave scouts, and scout leaders fair enough warning that the tale was not for everyone, especially the young first year Scout. It was the Scout Leaders call on who could, and who would not attend. The story intro is set to the Camp Rotary scene, and includes some actual history of the camp making it believable. One part in particular includes some graphic details while most of the tale just feeds the imagination. I've added some extra chapters over different summers taking it to about 90 minutes of story-telling. It is the most original tale that I've authored, and the most captive I've ever told. But reading it in this book isn't like hearing it in a camp fire setting. So, try to picture yourself on a dark night at Rotary, sitting beside the warmth of a fire. It's a clear night and the formations of stars are as beautiful as they can be as you watch, and hear the crackling of the burning wood giving out red, orange, and blue flames. The mood has been set as you brace yourself for the unexpected, and the scariest story ever told. Since 1998 it has been my signature.

HANNIBAL HAS ARRIVED
(Read by a scout or scouter).

Have you ever heard the phrase the only thing in life to fear is fear itself? Well, if you believe that, then you're in for a real shock because you are about to hear the legend of Camp Rotary's horrifying John Potter. The Hannibal has arrived! Now, you brave scouts, imagine this: it's in the wee hours of the morning, and you're bedded down in your tent. You are having a difficult time getting to sleep. You hear footsteps outside your tent. Whoever or whatever it is, it's breathing hard, and as the footsteps come closer, you start to slide further into your sleeping bag. You're sweating, and the liquidly beads are running down your back. Your heart's pounding rapidly. You pinch yourself thinking this must be a bad dream, "I'm just a kid, who'd want to hurt me?" You're too scared to scream, and your whole body's shaking as you hear your tent flap open, and the sound of the footsteps, and heavy breathing is now just inches from your bunk. Is it all a nightmare, or is it John, the Hannibal, Potter searching for a midnight snack?

"Fear not death, none but cowards fear to die," were the words spoken by Chippewa Chief Winnemucca in the mid 1800's on the property that is now Camp Rotary located in the central part of Michigan's lower peninsula. The camp has a beautiful spring-fed lake and fragrant pine trees on beautiful rolling hills, and is one of the most sought after camps in the nation. The property is rich in American Native lore. Native artifacts have been unearthed from the property over the years. The land was a great resource of lumber and black coal at the turn of the century. There's another side to Camp Rotary's history; evil occurrences that happened long ago, and now told to all to hear. This diabolical tale was passed down from an old settler in the area. He passed on to Waz a horrifying tale of a coal miner named John Potter, who was possessed by the devil himself. The settler asked Waz' not to reveal the tale to anyone. When he died, leaving Waz' with the horrible feats of John Potter, Waz couldn't keep the story to himself any longer. Thus the terrifying legend of John Potter was told for the first time.

It was in 1924 that the old Saginaw Council of the Boy Scouts of America first showed interest in Rotary's property which was owned by the Rotary Club of Saginaw. The property was home to large woodlands, much wildlife, and a large lake; great for fishing, swimming and boating. Many Native American artifacts were found while digging on the grounds. Historians tell us that the Shooting Sports range location was where Chief Winnemucca, and the Chippewa tribe met for pow-wows in the 1800's.

What you are about to hear, Waz is somewhat reluctant to tell. But it's part of the camp's history. We first must warn you, if you're lighthearted, and scare easily, adult or scout, then you might consider not listening to the legend of John, the Hannibal, Potter. This saga is not meant for 1ˢᵗ year scouts, and all scouts needed permission from their scout leaders to be here. Have you all gained that permission? You are about to hear the complete series of chapters, plus a brand new chapter which is the most terrifying of all. Everyone reacts differently to scary stories. Just don't say to yourself that you are not afraid to hear a tale that has gory, graphic details, and then in reality, deep down, you might be horrified. Therefore, I offer you one final warning, scouts, and scout Leaders, if you think that this story could interrupt your sleep tonight, now is your chance to leave this campfire. No one will think any less of you. Okay, don't say we didn't warn you, and if the story gets too much for anyone as we go along, you can leave during the story at any time. However, under no circumstance should anyone go back to their campsite without a buddy. If you want to leave, it would be best for you to stay in this campsite, out of hearing distance of the campfire, and wait for the story to end.

It was in the late 1800's, and early to mids-1900's, that mining for coal and cutting timber were the primary resources of income for this area. Lumbermen found giant pine trees towering the blue sky throughout the property. The lumberjacks or jacks as they were called were pleased to see the giant trees, some of which were five to six feet in diameter, and almost taller than the human eye could see. The trees were cut into logs, and the logs sent to the dam area on Beebe Lake, and from there floated down a large stream to Gladwin, Michigan, and continued down river to the Saginaw Bay, and Lake Huron in Bay City. When you are out and about, check the high ridge area immediately north of Curtis and James West Campsites, you'll see where the railroad tracks were located that transported the flat bed cars carrying the lumber to the dam. Coal production was also abundant. Under the ground on which we are above are coal mine tunnels and shafts, virtually under every campsite that have been vacant for many years. This story is of a coal miner who was a real person. His name was John Potter, alias the Hannibal. He lived just outside of the camp's property line, out by North Camp. From this moment on, I ask that there not be a sound coming from anyone. I suggest that you keep your flashlights on the ground between your feet, in the off positon. Fire tender, this will be your last opportunity to add wood to the campfire. It's important that everyone follow my instructions. It's important that no one disturbs this shocking tale. The legend of John Potter is the most terrifying, and horrifying tale ever. And now, here's a legend himself, telling campfire tales at Rotary since 1972, here's the Waz.

THE BEGINNING OF EVIL

John Potter was born to Will and Josephine Potter in 1927 in Clare, Michigan. Josephine Potter's pregnancy was not good. She nearly died on two occasions, and on a third occasion, when she finally gave birth, she died. The baby boy weighed almost 14 pounds, and was deformed. He had no lower lip, and only half of a nose, one nostril. Maybe it was a good thing that Josephine did not live to see her baby for he was truly gruesome to look at. Will Potter had a hard time accepting, and raising his son. He resented him for being born taking his wife's life. Will Potter wasn't a well man, and he definitely was not up to raising his son. He thought his son was the dumbest and ugliest child ever born. He often suspected, when John was a teenager, a teen that was very big, and large for his age, that he was the reason some of their livestock came up missing from the farm. But he wasn't sure of that; I mean, how could it be humanly possible for a young person, even as big as his son, to make large animals disappear? Well, Mr. Potter would never find out that John was indeed responsible for the disappearing animals, but that part of the story is yet to come. When John was 15 years old, his father suffered from deep depression, lost his mind, went mad, and was sent off to the home for the insane in Traverse City, Michigan.

John grew up just outside of Camp Rotary's property, out by North Camp. He did not go to school because most kids were afraid of him, and those who were not just made fun of him. We all know how kids can be. So, he worked his dad's farm, and stayed away from people as much as possible. But while working the farm, he couldn't help but notice young people, the scouts, inside Rotary's perimeter, hiking the trail by North Camp. Every now, and then a scout would look over to his direction through the property's fence line; noticed him, and run away terrified. John just stood there not doing anything to the scouts, but he scared them. One day, a scout spotted John, but he didn't yell, and run. He just pointed at him and laughed. The scout thought John's ugliness was funny. John didn't like anyone making fun of him. It made him wish that he never had been born. He didn't understand why kids had to be so mean. At 16 years of age, John was very tall, and strong; he was over six feet tall, and weighed nearly 300 pounds. He walked with a limp, and dragged his left foot because of a tractor accident that happened when he was 12 years old. If anyone walking through the woods came upon John, they would be truly horrified. John really didn't mean to scare anyone. He started out as a kind considerate person, especially to the animals of the forest, and even to children. It wasn't until later that something very terrible happened; he got hungry for them, very hungry. He discovered, at a younger age, that he had an appetite for the living, the young calves on the farm, and other creatures, especially, when he started venturing out in the evenings after dark. Because of his size, and features, he did not want anyone seeing him in the day light hours. Camp Rotary's property was John's domain. He was very comfortable in the night time setting as the deer, the bear, and other animals would come to him. He enjoyed feeding them, and picking them up, and petting them. Unfortunately, he never realized his own strength. He was so strong. His lust for the living started on one particular evening, while holding a small fawn, he squeezed it too hard, suffocating the small animal. It started to bleed as he watched some of its insides spilled to the ground. He had killed the poor animal. He fell to the ground, and cried, and cried. He did not mean any harm. But a strange feeling came over him. He fingered the blood, and guts lying on the ground, and took his fingers to his lips like taking a potato chip, and dipping it; then brought his fingers to his mouth, and the taste was very satisfying to him. This action was followed by him grabbing a solid piece of the flesh, and chewing on it. Then he swallowed it. With blood running down to his chin, he smiled, and gave out a hideous laugh that scared the other creatures in the forest. That night, in these woods, John became possessed by Satan, himself.

HIS VENTURE UNDER-GROUND

Later on, in August of 1945, when John was 18 years old, an opportunity came his way to work beneath the ground on Rotary's property, digging for coal. When the Saginaw Bay Council signed their lease with the Rotary Club of Saginaw, years ago, for the camp to be used as a summer resident scout camp, the council gave mining rights to a coal company to extract coal on the property; but only during the fall and winter months. John enjoyed being a coal miner because he worked mostly alone in the dark with a small light attached to his hard hat. It was a lot of bull work, but John was very strong. One unfaithful September day in 1945, the mine tunnel under Curtis Campsite, in which he was working, collapsed trapping him and two other co-workers. They were completely isolated from the other mining shafts on the camp's property, and out of the reach of other workers. They were able to survive by drinking water which seeped into the tunnel from Beebe Lake's underground spring. They also feasted on an abundance of wild mushrooms that they found. John knew that the mining company was not known for its compassion of its employees. However, he and his co-workers kept calling out for help while trying to dig out, and felt confident that others were digging from the outside in trying to rescue them. Actually the mining company never attempted to dig them out. The company figured all three of them had died. Back in the mine, John horrified the other two miners by catching live rats and eating them while they were still alive. The two miners were not doing well. When the mine collapsed, a large bolder fell on them crushing parts of their lower bodies. Gangrene had set in; they were running high fevers as the poison spread throughout their bodies. They were experiencing much pain, and then numbness as they both went into shock, then into comas, and died only minutes apart. What was John to do? Their flesh began to rot and smell. There was no place to bury them. The smell was too much for John. There was only one thing that John could do. He did the unthinkable, body part by body part. John eliminated the smell, body part by body part. John continued to dig as the weeks and months passed. During this time the mining company had gone bankrupted losing their mining lease to the Boy Scouts. Finally on November 23, 1945, while digging, John seen the sun light which temporarily blinded him. After 2 months, and 6 days, and 15 hours under the ground near James West Campsite, he finally managed to get out. John discovered that not one person had lifted a shovel to dig him out, and really lost it from being under the ground for so long. He began to feel his hunger pains like never before. He would take revenge, he promised. Revenge on anyone walking the grounds of Camp Rotary at night.

BODIES AND PARTS HERE, THERE, EVERYWHERE

Over the years bodies and bones have been found throughout Rotary's property. It's been hush, hush by the Clare County Sheriff's Department in order not to scare anyone off. The bodies found were bloody and torn. Close examination showed that they had teeth marks made by human teeth. One man was even beaten to death with his own arm, it was determined. And on July 27, 1955, the bodies of two men were found along the perimeter of Uncle Otto Campsite. They were beheaded and one was missing a leg. Two years later, an old hermit was found on the camp property by the old OA bowl. His body was badly decomposed and his eyes were missing. Anyone walking in the woods at night seems to be fair game for John who was now labeled the Hannibal by the folks living in the area. Back then, whenever the authorities tried to find him, he would somehow disappear. It was thought that he could be hiding in one of the many vacant mine tunnels throughout the camp that he knew so well. Anyway, since 1957 no further bodies were discovered until the summer of 1974. Three scouts digging a footing for a monkey bridge over at Braden Campsite found a human skull, and the skeleton remains of three others. They were identified as three Scout Leaders who were reported missing during the summer of 1968. Two leaders were from the Detroit Area Council, and one from the Blue Water Council. And in December of 1975 over at Ranger Campsite, much to the dismay of the police, they found the remains of two much smaller skeletons. It was what the authorities had feared the most, John's first Boy Scout victims. Two scouts, a 12 year old from Bloomfield Hills and a 14 year old from Farmington, MI. They were reported missing in July of 1970. Then just two days later a much smaller skeleton was found at Baden-Powell Campsite. A Scout was digging a hole for the campsite's flag pole when he discovered it. It was the partial remains of a Cub-Scout from Sterling Heights who was reported missing in July of 1968 while camping with his dad on a Lad and Dad week-end campout. Police were at a dead-end. Bodies were being discovered, but John Potter wasn't. No other bodies have been discovered since December of 1975; however, the Sheriff believes that there are more remains yet to be found because of human bone fragments that have been spotted throughout the camp. Parts of humans have been discovered as recently as 2003, and 2009, and 2012. In March of 2003, a first class Scout from a troop in Milford, MI., found a human foot bone floating over by the bridge going to Fort Scott, and North Camp. In 2009 another scout from Bay City, MI. reported seeing a part of a skeleton 12 feet deep in Lake Beebe close to the swimmers area. And again in 2012, over by the dam area, a scout from Flint, Michigan, who was fishing, caught a 21 inch large-mouth bass. When he cleaned his trophy fish, he found a human toe inside its cavity. Law enforcement officials still continue to search for John Potter, and are puzzled that he has never been seen. Some figured he must have died while others figure he's still alive. If he is, he would be well into his 90's. I should think that anyone could out run a 90 year old man, right? So, should we consider ourselves safe or not?

A PLEA FROM A CAMP DIRECTOR

Before we decide that, you should first hear what this affidavit says. This is a legal document signed by Camp Rotary's previous Camp Director. "On the morning of November 17, 2005, I spotted a small black bear at Fort Scott. The bear seem to be confused, and running in a circle. I observed it to be foaming from the mouth. I took my 12 gauge, and put two slugs through its heart. I discovered that the dead bear was rabies infected, and noticed on the bear's neck two large penetration wounds made by human teeth. I also discovered some very large human footprints in the area. I must insist that all scouts, and leaders heed my instructions; always use the buddy system when traveling on camp property especially after dark, and never be in your tent alone at night." This affidavit was signed and dated, November 18, 2005. Well, what about it? Some of you scouts probably refuse to believe in John Potter, right? Well, what I'm about to tell is the gospel truth. In this very campsite, almost a year to this very date, the scout leaders and scouts reported someone walking very slowly through the campsite around 2 A.M. Whoever or whatever it was, it was dragging something. Everyone was afraid, and didn't leave their bunks to investigate. The walking, and dragging continued for the longest time. Also, last year, during the 5th week of summer camp, again in this very campsite, Troop 2234 was camping here. It was raining that night. The scouts just had a campfire followed by a cracker barrel, and then went to their tents. There were two scouts in that tent over there, the one closest to the road that heard the noise first. One of the scouts was so tired; he just went to sleep leaving the other scout awake. The scout heard a rumpus just outside his tent, and slid down into his sleeping bag hoping it would go away. But the noise wouldn't leave. He kept calling out to his sleeping buddy, but it was useless, his buddy was motionless. Now he heard a moaning sound, and this time yelled to his buddy, "Wake up, please wake up, there's something outside our tent!" He heard his tent flap flapping. He was too afraid to peek as he slid deeper, and deeper into this sleeping bag covering his head. He was shaking, and really scared; he thought he might wet his bed. The tent flapping continued, and although he could not see, he felt the presence of someone or something standing by his bunk. Above him came that moaning noise again. He tried to scream but could not. Beads of sweat ran down his face and body. His whole bed was shaking; he was horrified beyond words as he now felt his sleeping bag being touched. He passed out. The Scout woke up in the morning telling his buddy that he had a bad dream. As they were putting their uniforms on, his buddy reminded him of the buddy system, and asked why he went to the latrine alone last night. He answered that he did not go to the bathroom at all, and why would he asked that. His tent buddy replied, "Well look at the muddy footprints on the ground going towards your bunk." He looked downward towards the ground and gave a terrifying "YIKES!"

"I THINK I SAW HIM AT MY CAMPSITE!"

I have another affidavit, a legal document from an Eagle Scout, Scout Alex Neiman of Troop 116 from Richmond, Virginia. Alex and his troop camped at Rotary during summer camp, 2010. This is his sworn statement: "To everyone camping at Camp Rotary. Hi, my name is Alex Neiman of Troop 116. My troop camped at Daniel Boone Campsite. We had a great week at Rotary. The rappelling tower was the coolest, and COPE was a blast along with swimming, rifle and shotgun. I need to talk to you on a serious happening. Yeah, you guessed it, John Potter. I got to tell you guys, years ago when I first heard the story, it completely freaked me out. Good grief! Even though it's hard to believe, it sure gives you the chills. Now I have to admit, some stuff in the story is pretty gruesome, and I think, on the other hand, really cool. At first I didn't' think much of the story. I mean let's get real, a big 300 pound ugly dude walking the woods at night, tearing off the flesh of live people, and eating them. I mean how true can that be? Hannibal's only in the movies, right? Someone in Hollywood made him up, right? Well, I originally thought so, but I got to tell you that I'm looking at things differently now, and it really sucks. Why? Well, I think I saw the big ugly dude in my campsite at Boone, and then one time out by North Camp. Now you don't have to believe me, but I'm not making this up, and my intentions are not to frighten you, only to warn you. Truthfully, you really need to be on your guard, especially after dark. When you think about it, all scout camps across the United States are supposed to be safe havens for youth. So, why didn't anyone tell us about Rotary's John Potter? The only answer I can come up with is, if they had, who would ever camp at Camp Rotary, right? Now, I've given much thought to Waz's story, and even though it's hard to believe, when you think about it, it's pretty cool that there have been Sasquatch sightings in every part of the world. Down south, we call him Skunk Man. But most folks just call him Big Foot, and here we are in Clare, Michigan with our very own Yeti who goes by the name of John Potter. Anyway, besides spotting him at North Camp from a distance one evening, I believe I had a close encounter with the beast at Boone Campsite. It was on a Wednesday evening, and an extremely hot night in the campsite. I had just attended a patrol leaders meeting. I'm patrol leader of the Dragons. I was getting ready for bed. I slept in a tent just like yours with my buddy, Chad. By the way, do you trust your tent buddy? I mean would he come through for you in an emergency? Well, my tent partner is just plain worthless. As soon as he hits the bed, he's out of the picture. I tried to wake him once by blowing my bugle next to his bunk. He never budged. It was about midnight, I had a hard time getting to sleep, it was really hot, and Chad was snoring very loud as usual. Since it was so humid, I placed my mattress on the floor, and tossed, and turned. It was around 2 A.M., I think, that I started to doze off. That is until I took a glance at the tent flap opening. There I saw a tall, large figure of something peeking into the tent. I froze. It had quite a large torso, and kept looking in the tent. I tried not to make a sound or movement, but I did whisper to Chad, and you know how well that worked out. Then I got enough courage to turn on the mattress with my back to the opening of the tent, hoping it would leave. I knew it could not have been a normal person, but I didn't want to believe that John Potter was watching. Now, scouts, if you stare at anything long enough in the darkness, you will sense movement. Well, all I could visualize in the darkness of the early morning hours was John Potter with those big teeth of his coming into my tent to tear off my flesh, and eat me. Now, I'm a Boy Scout, and trying to be calm and brave (after all we're supposed to be brave, right?), I began to think that there are times in one's life when we must summon every shred of courage to stand tall and steady in the face of fear. Therefore, would I be a true knight in the tradition of the round table of old or would I be a WIMP? And with the thought in mind, I stuck out my chest, took a deep breath, and decided a wimp I would be. And from deep within my lungs gave out the loudest scream, and ran out through the other side of my tent, and kept running until I reached my Scoutmaster's, Mr. Johnson's tent. I must have had really scared him, because he yelled, and jumped up so high, he hit his head on the top ridge pole to the tent. Now, scouts, I have to tell you, whenever you're afraid of the night or have any fears, never be reluctant to wake up your scoutmaster. He is the bravest amongst all scout leaders. Together, Mr. Johnson, and I walked back to my tent. Chad was sound asleep. Why didn't that surprise me? Mr. Johnson thought I had a nightmare of sorts. It wasn't a nightmare. It was real. About 4 A.M., the moon was partially full and we were both still standing outside when we heard something stirring in the bushes. We both stood steadfast, and then heard a cracking noise from a nearby tree branch. "Deer, right?" I asked Mr. Johnson. "Probably," he replied. Then we heard the same sound again, but this time it was much louder. I said, "That wasn't a little branch; that was something much bigger." Mr. Johnson interrupted, "Now don't let your imagination run from you, son." Mr. Johnson didn't want to admit it, but he was feeling almost as much anxiety as I. I thought to myself, what's ever out there is bigger; bigger as in Big Foot or worse, bigger as in John Potter. Chad was the only one left undisturbed that night. I didn't get much sleep, and neither did Mr. Johnson. When I returned home from Rotary, I didn't tell my parents of my experience. I should have had, but I didn't want to frighten them. But you need to take my warning seriously. I believe that John Potter, the Hannibal, is among us. So be on your guard, your life could depend on it. That particular week at Rotary was the most terrifying time in my life, ever."

SIGNED: Alex Neimann, Troop 116, July 2010, Camp Rotary

OLD JOES' ENCOUNTER

Back in 2011 on October 12th, I was in the Camp Office visiting with the Camp Director. He had a visitor that he introduced me to, an elderly gentleman. His name was Joseph Prime who went by "Old Joe." He said that he camped at Rotary as a youngster back in the late 40's and early 50's. I found "Old Joe" to be a very colorful person, who had lots of tales to share about Rotary. After some great conversation, I came right out and asked him of John Potter. I asked if all the reports of Potter were true. He didn't answer me right off, he kept changing the subject. But I remained persistent, and kept going back to my original question. He motioned me to the office door, and together we walked out to the parking lot towards Schuck Campsite. We were both silent for a while; I was waiting for him to make the first move. He gave out a deep breath and said, "Now, what I'm about to say, like the old saying goes, whatever happens in camp, stays in camp." I said that I would not take whatever he was about to say to anyone else. He continued, "Whatever you heard of John Potter is probably factual, he's really a bad-butt." I responded, "Well, Old Joe, how do you know that?" Because," he returned, "I have actually seen body parts in camp by the old sewer pond next to the dining hall." My anxiety was on a rise, and what he said next, really floored me, "And there's more, I actually had an encounter with the demon late one night in Schuck Campsite." Startled, I came back with, "You mean you seen him face to face?" "Yep'er," he replied. "Well, what did you do, run?" I asked. "What any young scout would do, I went number one, and two in my pants, I was scared out of my wits," he said. "Well, did he come after you?" I asked. "No," he replied, "he just stared at me with those big eyes on that really ugly face of his for the longest time, and then walked away going in one direction, and I in the other. Except I didn't walk, I ran! Maybe he wasn't hungry at that moment, I don't know, and I don't care. I just count my blessings that I'm here to tell you this today." "Good grief," I responded with a dropped jaw. He went on to say, "That's why I never ever come to this camp in the evening. I never want another experience like that again. It has stayed with me all these years, and I can't let it go." I never forgot that meeting with Old Joe. His face to face encounter with John "The Hannibal" Potter had to be an experience that none of us will ever want.

A SCOUT'S NIGHTMARE, BUT HE WASN'T SLEEPING

It was late Wednesday evening. Zack and Brandon were first class scouts, and had a very busy day of summer camp. Zack had a full load of merit badges behind him; swimming, boating, canoeing, camping and cooking. Brandon had a busy day also with a similar schedule. They both were very close to their Star Ranks, and although they were very tired, tonight was going to be a special one with a very special campfire. Eagerly, they had waited all week for the Waz to show up to tell his story of the Legend of John Potter, the horror story that they had heard so much about. When Waz arrived, and warned everyone about the scary tale, Zach and Brandon just laughed to themselves. Waz went through the whole story, and when he was done, everyone was dumbfounded for it was truly a scary tale, and they really didn't know how much truth there was to it. But now it was late in the evening, and they were too exhausted to be scared. They just wanted to hit their bunks. Inside their tent, lying on their sleeping gear, Zack asked Brandon, "You know, you just can't believe in John, the

Hannibal Potter. I think Waz made it all up. Who can believe in a big guy like that going around eating people?" Brandon replied, "You're right. It can't be true. I think Waz just enjoys scaring scouts." With that, Brandon slipped into a deep sleep really fast. It took Zach a little longer to fall into his coma. From his bunk, he peered through the tent flap opening into a beautiful summer evening. The formations of stars were as beautiful, and bright as they could be. He thought about an arrow head that he held in his hand. He had found it at the rifle range. "At least that part of the John Potter story is true," He told himself, "There are Indian things buried in camp, and I do remember my scoutmaster telling us about finding some human bones in camp. But they were thought to be from a couple of deer hunters who died from the cold, many winters ago." Zach's eye lids became heavy, and he finally drifted off to sleep. It was a very warm evening, and there was a strong aroma coming from the pine trees nestled around their campsite. The moon was a full one. There was a dog barking in the distance along with the sound of a train on its tracks. About 1 A.M., nothing was moving about, not even the raccoons or chipmunks running from tent to tent, and that was very unusual. Where were those critters, those critters of the evening? There was a little breeze this night that would shake the ridge poles, and canvas to the tent from time to time. But it wasn't enough of a problem to wake up these two sleepy heads, Zach and Brandon. And then from the camp road, came footsteps, heavy ones, moving through the brush towards Zach's and Brandon's tent. "WHAT WAS THAT?!" Yelled Zach as he sat up in his bunk motioning to his tent partner, "Brandon, did you hear that?" Brandon did not budge; he was in tri-light land. The noise was coming closer to the tent. He checked the tent zipper making sure the canvas was zipped shut. They were indeed footsteps, heavy ones, made by someone or something really big. Zach slid deeper into his sleeping bag covering his whole body. His heart was pounding hard as he pinched himself thinking, "This must be a nightmare. I'm just a kid, who would want to hurt me?" Then he popped his head out of the sleeping bag, and yelled to the top of his lungs towards Brandon, but Brandon still did not move. He pleaded, "Please, please, Brandon, please wake up. I hear footsteps outside the tent and whoever it is, it's dragging something, and I'm really scared!" Now he heard the footsteps, along with the terrifying dragging, just outside the door to the tent. Again, he tried to slide deeper into his sleeping bag. He closed his eyes wishing that he was home in the safety of his own bed. Whispering out loud to himself, "Mom, Dad, please help me, make it go away, I miss your guys, and I'm really scared." He began to cry as he now heard the zipper being pulled opened, and the footsteps enter the tent. He heard heavy breathing just above his head. He would not open his eyes. He began praying, and pretended being elsewhere, like in his backyard at home jumping on his trampoline. It didn't do any good; he could not escape the terror that he was experiencing, as he now heard a moaning sound just inches away. He was trembling; he made tight fists with both hands, and crutched them against the cheeks of his face as tight as he could. His legs and feet gave way to uncontrollable kicking. Then inside his sweat soaked sleeping bag, he felt as though he was being lifted from his bunk.

WOW! IT DOESN'T GET ANY SCARIER THAN THIS!

It was about 8 A.M., Zach woke up on this particular morning, and wondered why his parents permitted him to over-sleep since it was a school day. He opened his bedroom door and called, "Mom, Dad, anyone there?" There was no response. As he got dressed, he thought back to Camp Rotary, and all the fun he had; climbing, repelling, swimming and canoeing. And boy, did he enjoy being a patrol leader in the troop, "I'm a good leader and hopefully the guys will elect me as their next senior patrol leader." He finished dressing, and while sitting on the edge of his bed, he felt a little dizzy. He just didn't feel right. It was like he was in a daze, and couldn't focus. He definitely was experiencing something far from the norm. He ran downstairs to the kitchen. No one was there, and neither was his little sister, Kaylee, or younger brother, Jason. No one was at home. It was weird. He checked the garage and noticed his Dad's Chevrolet was gone. "Now, why would they leave me home alone like this?" he asked himself. He felt some dizziness coming on again, and sat at the kitchen table. He looked up to the kitchen ceiling fan, and on its own, it started to turn in a circular direction, and then the kitchen walls started to rotate in the opposite direction. He closed his eyes. Faster and faster, the room, and fan rotated. With his eyes shut, it felt as though he was riding on an out-of-control speeding merry-go-round, and he just couldn't make it stop. He also felt extremely cold, with no feeling to his feet, and arms, and hands. After a time, another strange feeling came over him, like he was being lifted out of his own body. Then he thought he heard voices, lots of them. The dizziness stopped, he opened his eyes, and shockingly, he found that he was no longer in the kitchen. He was at an outdoor setting, among trees, and green grass. He had no idea what was going on, or where he was. He questioned himself, "This can't be happening to me. I'm losing my mind." But the voices he heard were coming from a large group of people standing in a semi-circle. He saw his Mother and Father. Running to them, he yelled, "Mom, Dad, what's going on?" Crying, they looked at Zach but didn't respond to him. He kept talking to them, but it was as if they could not hear him, and were looking through him. His little sister, and brother, at their parent's side, was crying also. He put his arms around them to hug them, and when he did, he could not feel their bodies. It seem like Kaylee, and Jason were looking through him.. He yelled, "Sis, Jason, it's me your big brother, Zach, please see me!" He noticed many other familiar faces in the crowd; all of his relatives including Grandma and Grandpa, and his friends, and neighbors were there. His 8th grade class and teacher were there including his girlfriend, Tanya. All of them, every last one of them were crying. They were weeping over an opened grave with a coffin sitting by it, being readied to be lowered. He saw his troop and scoutmaster; all in uniform saluting. He ran to them, "Hey, guys it's me, Zach!" There was no response. His scoutmaster, with tears running down his cheeks, was talking to another adult at his side, "I can't believe Zach is gone. He was the nicest young man with a bright future ahead of him. His life has been cut short. And the way he died; mutilated like he was. Then for the authorities to find his body at Rotary just two months after he was reported missing." The other adult replied, "Yeah, his body was badly decomposed. The animals must have had a field day on him. If it wasn't for the DNA samples, the CSI unit would never have learned it was the body of 13 year old Zach. He was precious young man, a real leader, who excelled in school and sports. He wanted to attend the University of Michigan like his dad." Zach was in disbelief, and complete shock. Then he saw his pastor from church hand a handkerchief to his Mom and Dad. He was saying, "Dust to dust, ashes to ashes. We commend the body of...." "Hold, it! Hold, it!"

Zach, screamed out as loud as he could as he watched the coffin being lowered into the grave. He ran back to his Mom, and Dad, and siblings tripping over something on the ground. It was a grave marker bearing his engraved name. Lying on the ground, he cried out as loud as he could, "Mom, Dad, I'm not dead, I'm here. I love you guys, more than anything in the world. I don't want to be dead!" The more he pleaded, the more he cried, "Mom, Dad, I don't want to be dead!"

THE AFTERMATH

"Zack, Zack, Zack! Wake up, son. Why are you crying so? Look at you, you're a wash cloth, your blanket and pillow, they're soaking wet. What's going on, son?" It was his Mother's voice, "You had a bad dream, Zack." Zack was dazed. Rubbing his eyes, and sitting up in bed, he asked, "Am I dead, Mom?" "Don't be silly now, and get dress, it's almost 8 0'Clock, you'll be late for the school bus," his Mother directed. Zack hugged his Mother so tightly that she had a hard time breaking his grip. As he got dressed for school, his thoughts ran back to summer camp, "Bad dream, Mom says, boy that's an understatement. Who would ever have thought that Waz's John Potter story would have affected me like it has? I'll never listen to another scary story in my life! YOU HEAR THAT, WAZ', NEVER!" Downstairs in the kitchen, he caught his little sister and brother by surprise and hugged them. They were puzzled with his rare act of affection, and couldn't push him away fast enough. On the school bus, he laughed, and joked with his classmates. As the bus pulled into the school yard, Zack smiled, and quickly got off, and headed to the doors of the school, thinking, "Boy, it's great to be alive!"

YOU DON'T BELIEVE IN JOHN POTTER, DO YOU?

In the book "Kepayshowink," written by Normal Scheall, she describes Camp Rotary as a dynamic Scout camp with rolling hills and fragrant pine trees and a beautiful lake. It's very easy to be captured in its surroundings especially watching the sun as it sets, and hearing the cry of the loon or feeling the tug of a large mouth on your fishing line. Walking the many trails around camp, you'll see prints made by critters of different sizes, and hear their sounds, and those of the birds, the trees and the lake. I call it the sights and sounds of the present, all having a magic to them, for they help us visualize the sights, and sounds of the past; a reminder of a horrifying, and terrifying past, because some folks have witnessed, throughout the years, some very large human foot prints that can't be explained. John Potter was or is a factual being. In the book of an early settler in Clare County, "The Story of Spike Horn" by T. M. Sellers, it mentions a John Potter being murdered many years ago in Clare, Michigan. He was shot to death by a Native American name Red Eagle. Now, a few folks don't believe that, because there's speculation that John Potter's body never found its' way to the city morgue. So, if John Potter is alive today, he would be very old. But I guess his age would not prevent him stalking the woods, because some believe that he still does. Now, I offer everyone a word of caution. After you're bedded down for the evening, safely in your tent, think about this, and ask yourself, "What's that noise I heard outside the tent?" And then you hear footsteps coming towards your tent, and you see your tent flaps open; then out of the darkness of night, in your tent, you sense movement. Well, Scouts, there are options that one can take. You could sleep with one eye open, and I don't know of any human that can do that. Or you can take turns with your tent buddy, one scout sleeps while the other keeps watch, because falling asleep together might not be a good thing to do. Then again, maybe all of it could just by your imagination running away from you; because deep down, you really don't believe in John "the Hannibal" Potter, or do you?

THE DISCLAIMER

Scouts, the story you just heard, I wrote. Aside from a few factual accounts of Camp Rotary's history, the story is fiction. In the storyline, names of characters are fictional as well as any associated troop numbers; cities and states. There are no coal mines at Rotary. There are no tunnels, no mine shafts. There never was. The terrifying events that I described in the story line never happened. I got the idea for this story from the Hannibal movies. The title came to me from the Harry Potter books. I thought Potter would be a good name to remember. In the Spike Horn Meyer's book, there was a real John Potter who was murdered in Clare County back in the early 1900's, before my fictional John Potter came along. I found out about the real John Potter after I titled my story. There is no connection between my fictional John Potter, and the real John Potter. The real John Potter did die, and he's long gone, and the John, the Hannibal, Potter, whom I made-up, never existed. The story of John, the Hannibal, Potter, and his terrible deeds are from my imagination. It's all make-believe, so you have nothing to fear. Sleep tight, and thanks for coming, and let your dreams be happy ones.

"WAZZZUUUP!"

"….In and among the various magnificent stands of trees, firmly rooted and grounded in the gently rolling countryside of this scared place, visitors have the privilege of experiencing, first hand, God's exhilarating, loving presence……It's mysterious, spiritually-renewing and awe-inspiring qualities, which left a profoundly positive impact on most everyone who has spent a part of their lives in this entrancing and joy-filled camp, will, God willing, always be available for future generations to enjoy."

Rev. Fr. Frederick R. Engdahl, Jr.
Former Camp Rotary Staffer

Photographs

All photographs used in this book are the property of the author with the exception of those listed below:

"Scouts Canoeing on Beebe Lake 1956"	Erwin M. Hutter ©2014
"Camp Rotary Front Gate 1978"	ibid.
2 photos of the Hutter boys at Camp Rotary Campfire Bowl 1972	ibid.
"Mischigonong Lodge Chief Erv Hutter-1979"	©1979 Mark I Photography
Andrew Wright at Valentine Amphitheater 2013	©Andrew Wright 2013.
Marv and Justine Valentine about 1982	©M. B. Valentine 2014.
Marv and Justine Valentine Wedding Day 1953	©M.B. Valentine 2014.
Marvin B. Valentine	©M.B. Valentine 2014.
Marv Valentine and Mark Sprygada 1997	©Erwin M. Hutter 1997.
Marv Valentine 1979	©Erwin M. Hutter 1979.
Valentine Amphitheater	©Erwin M. Hutter 2011.
Marvin B. Valentine about 1985	©M. B. Valentine 2014.

"The Good Ole' Days of Camp"

"Remember when we needed to keep the scouts occupied, it was always Capture the Flag?"

"Who doesn't remember going on a Snipe Hunt?"

"Or how about fetching a left-handed monkey wrench or sky-hook? Remember climbing the old water tower?"

"Remember the long lines to the pay-phone outside the camp's office?"

"Or being stuck in the basement for hours and hours because of a tornado warning?"

"On a stormy-rainy night, sleeping in those so called, water-proof, Voyager tents?"

"When having S.O.S. for breakfast?"

"The staff pizza parties on Thursday evenings at North Camp?"

"Remember the Water Carnival competition on Saturdays?"

"Or star gazing on the parade field – no better place to do it?"

"Collecting those M-T pop cans throughout the summer to pay for the end of summer staff party?"

"Those extra-large critter's tracks, out by the dam?"

"Remember "Sloppy-Joe" Sundays?"

"The Staff pool games in the basement?"

"Remember Sponge-Bob entraining us in the dining hall?"

"The $1.98 Beauty Contest and the Gong-Show?"

"This is the song that never ends?"

"Remember the ever popular obstacle course at SCSC along with the gigantic monkey bridge?"

"Or the scouts competing, climbing the grease pole, and the hole- in-one putting competition at the Wednesday carnival where we actually barbequed a whole pig?"

"Remember those "Good-Scout Awards" being presented at evening colors? And driving those golf balls into the lake?"

"And, Where Oh Where is Susie?"

About the Authors

Richard A. "WAZ" Wasmer is a native of Midland Park, New Jersey. He is a United States Air Force veteran and a life-long Scouter, having served with the Trans-Atlantic Council, BSA, in Europe and North Africa. He is a retiree of the Dow Chemical Company in Midland, Michigan and Bangor Township Schools and resides in Bay City, Michigan, with his wife Kathy. For more than 50 years, Waz has served in numerous capacities in scouting. He has served Camp Rotary for over four decades, mostly as a Camp Commissioner; as a Program Director, and Assistant Camp Director. He also served as Program Director and Assistant Camp Director at the former Lost Lake Scout Reservation in Lake, Michigan. He is the founding Scoutmaster of Troop 103 in Bay City. He is a Vigil Honor member of the Order of the Arrow, a recipient of the Founder's Award and a former Chapter Advisor. He is active in his church and community, and is a Past Grand Knight of Council #414, Knights of Columbus in Bay City. He is a strong supporter of Camp Rotary.

Rev. Erwin M. "Erv" Hutter is a native of Bay City, Michigan. He is a graduate of T. L. Handy High School, Delta College, Saginaw Valley State College and Concordia Seminary. He an Eagle Scout from Troop 119 in Bay City. He is a former Lodge Chief of Mischigonong Lodge and a Vigil Honor

member. He has served on Boy Scout summer camp staffs for 15 summers including 10 of those summers at Camp Rotary. He is the founder and president of the Camp Rotary Staff Association and a member of the Camp Rotary Properties and Program Committees. He has served in numerous scouting positions throughout the Midwest on the unit, district and council levels. He is an ordained Lutheran pastor and lives with his wife Dawn and children Christian, Katie, and Andy in Taylor, Michigan. He is a member of the Society of George and a strong supporter of Camp Rotary.

Andrew T. Wright is a native of Bay City, Michigan, and a graduate of All Saints High School and Central Michigan University. He is a Vigil Honor member of the Order of the Arrow. He is an Eagle Scout from Troop 111 in Bay City. He has served on camp staff at Camp Rotary for over a decade and in October 2014 was named the 34th Camp Director of Camp Rotary (since 1926). Andrew lives at camp year-round with his new bride Jelina.

Troop 134, Larry Jeziorski, Scoutmaster, Bloomfield Hills, Michigan, receiving the Silver Axe Award, summer camp.1995

There will be happiness, and at times, pain and suffering in any direction we travel. In His plan, God is always there for us showing us how to "walk the walk" in good times as well as the bad. And in the bad, He helps us to find the strength; the strength to move on.

"WAZZZUUP!"